IMAGES OF ENGLAND

STOCKPORT

Stockport rooftops from High Bankside, February 1969. The electricity works 'tower' and chimney have since been demolished.

IMAGES OF ENGLAND

STOCKPORT

MORRIS GARRATT AND SHIRLEY McKENNA

The
History
Press

First published in 1999 by Tempus Publishing
Reprinted 2001

Reprinted in 2011 by
The History Press
The Mill, Brimscombe Port,
Stroud, Gloucestershire, GL5 2QG
www.thehistorypress.co.uk

ISBN 978 0 7524 1128 6

Typesetting and origination by
Tempus Publishing Limited
Printed and bound in Great Britain.

Looking towards Warren Street from what is now the top end of the Merseyway Precinct,
probably in the late 1960s. The mill and the buildings in the background were swept away to
make way for the Warren Street development. This metal 'sculpture', proclaiming that this is
Merseyway, was a prominent feature at that time – no one seems to know what happened to it!

Contents

This photograph is comparatively recent – it dates from the early 1970s – and shows a view of Stockport Parish Church. However, change has already taken place since these recent times, as the shops at the right were demolished in the mid-1970s. Thatcher's bakers still trade elsewhere in the town.

Introduction

For all its proximity to its larger neighbour Manchester – six miles away along the A6 – Stockport (previous spellings include Stopford, Stopport, Stockford and others) remains today what it has always been: a Cheshire market town and a focus of activity for the surrounding districts. Historically its origins are lost in the mists of time, but the archaeological evidence suggests that the area was inhabited certainly by the Bronze Age. We need not dwell on its historical development in any detail – that has been done by Heginbotham (*Stockport Ancient and Modern:* 2 vols, 1888 and 1892) and, even while this book was in preparation, most satisfactorily by Peter Arrowsmith (*Stockport: A History*, 1997). Suffice it to say that by the thirteenth century the Barony of Stockport – a barony signifies the control of a number of manors by a single lord – was in existence, the Lordship being held by the de Stokeport family. It has long been accepted that Robert de Stokeport, the second of that name, granted the inhabitants a Borough Charter dating from around 1220. The original charter has not survived, the copy in existence being made in 1530. Recent thinking seems to suggest that the Borough Charter may be more nearly contemporary with the Market Charter of 1260, which was granted by Prince Edward, Earl of Chester, to the third Robert de Stokeport and gave the Borough permission to hold a weekly market and an annual fair. The granting of these two charters provided the impetus for the subsequent development of the town.

A sandstone Parish Church was built in the late thirteenth or early fourteenth century, and the Grammar School was founded in 1487 by the will of Sir Edmund Shaa. The town became a Municipal Borough in 1835, and a County Borough in 1894. The population increased dramatically, from 14,000 in 1800 to 33,000 by 1821; by 1835 it had reached 44,666. The population of the Parliamentary Borough was 70,263 in 1891, and 127,000 by 1935.

Even before local government reorganization in 1974, Stockport had already absorbed a number of the smaller surrounding townships: Reddish and a part of Cheadle in 1901, Heaton Norris Urban District in 1913, Offerton detached from Hazel Grove in 1935, and part of Brinnington in 1952. The Metropolitan Borough created in 1974 incorporated several previously independent townships, some of which have already warranted their own individual book in the *Archive Photographs* Series: *Marple and Mellor*, and *Hazel Grove and Bramhall*. We have, therefore, confined ourselves to the area of the pre-1974 Borough.

Readers may feel that the appearance of yet another book of photographs of Stockport in times past might seem like a case of 'overkill' in a market already well provided for. However, new and previously untapped sources are always becoming available, and we have no reason to suppose that this book will be the last! The list of acknowledgements indicates the many sources, both public and private, from which previously unpublished material has been retrieved, even in an already well documented place like Stockport. Topics such as transport (railways, tramways and buses) and industries as diverse as aircraft, hatting and textiles have been dealt with in detail elsewhere, though clearly we could not totally ignore them. We have, in general, tried to avoid the more familiar and well used pictures of Stockport while at the same time recognizing that sources like Heginbotham, for example, although long out of print, contain images still important to the town's history, and we have used a few of these.

All local historians have difficulty in keeping abreast of redevelopment and alterations as older streets and their buildings are obliterated by motorways and bypasses, supermarkets, shopping precincts, industrial and new housing estates – and car parks! Names, locations and events have all been the subject of much detailed research, although changes of street names, in-fill building causing renumbering, and sometimes the inadequacy and lack of continuity of local directories have all caused problems.

All of the postcard images included have been examined minutely using a magnifying glass – something we would recommend everyone to try – you never know what you might see! In a number of cases, as especially exemplified in the case of Tom Potts' wedding (see p. 61), the postmark and/or the message can be as important as the photograph itself.

We have also used some of the prints taken from slides and photographs in the Stockport Historical Society's Cyril Warren Collection, which he put together from the mid-1960s until his death in 1978. As some of the sources of these have not been traced – Cyril copied a lot of material borrowed from various libraries, friends and people he met through his local history talks – we apologise if we have not acknowledged the owners for their use. We are most grateful to the many members and friends of the Stockport Historical Society who have provided material for this present work, and not least to the generations of anonymous photographers who, perhaps unwittingly, have contributed to a continuing pictorial history of our town.

Acknowledgements

We have mentioned our indebtedness to Heginbotham and Arrowsmith above. It is our very great pleasure to record here the names of all those individuals and organizations who have helped us, either by the loan of their material or with additional information, and in one case at least to avoid an embarrassing situation!

We must first thank the Executive Committee of the Stockport Historical Society for granting us access to the collection built up by the late Cyril Warren and which is in the Society's care. We are also indebted to: Ms Lynne Ranson, Mr David Reid and the staff of the Local Heritage Library, Stockport Central Library for their assistance and knowledge so freely shared, Miss Janet Bailey, Mrs Vivian Bath, Mr Alan Crossley, Mrs Anita Cutler, Miss Doris Dean, Mrs Joyce Embrey, Miss M. Gilbody, the late Mr Tom Goodwin, Mr Malcolm Harmer, Mr J. Peter Harrison, Mr Graham Hyland, Mrs Sylvia Hill, Mrs Beryl Hubble, Mr Martin Johnson, Mrs Maureen Jones, Mrs Linda Lewis formerly of Edgeley and now in Australia, Ms Audrey Linkman at the Documentary Photography Archive, Ms A. Lock at Tameside Local Studies Library, Manchester Central Library, Mrs Pauline Morris, Mrs Enid Price, Mr John Price, the late Mr Fred Ridgway, Mrs Charlotte Riggs, Mr E. Alan Rose, Mr Roger G. Simpson, Dr J.H. Smith, Mr R.E.G. Smith, Mr Tony Steele, Mrs Joan Thomas, Miss Audrey C. Walsh, Miss Dorothy Westhead, the late Mrs Edna Wyatt. Our thanks also go to Mr Derek Seddon for his excellent photographic work. Finally we must thank our respective partners, Mrs Eileen Garratt and Mr Alan McKenna, for putting up with the inconvenience and disruption to their normal way of life!

M.G. and S.M.

One

In and Around the Market Place

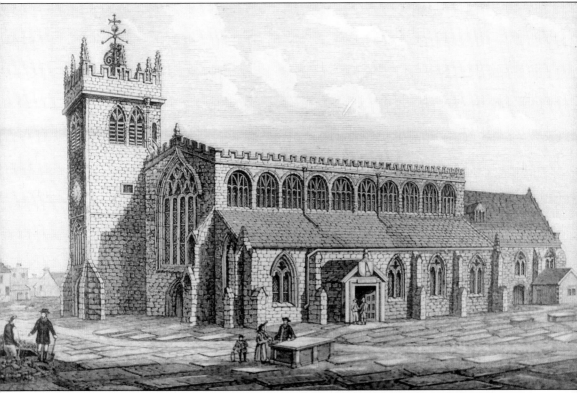

The Parish Church of St Mary the Virgin (to quote its full name) from an illustration from Heginbotham. In Saxon times Stockport may have had a wooden church, of which no trace has so far been found. After the Norman Conquest a small sandstone church was built to serve a large parish which stretched from Dukinfield to Disley. In the fifteenth century, the north and south aisles and a clerestory were added. An existing tower and steeple were rebuilt between 1612 and 1617, but the steeple fell in 1714 and was not replaced. The illustration shows the old church as it must have looked prior to 1810, when all but the chancel was demolished. The church was rebuilt to the designs of Lewis Wyatt. The foundation stone for the new church was laid on 5 July 1813. It seats 2,000 people and was consecrated on 4 July 1817. The new tower was 125ft high and the new nave, encased in Runcorn stone, rests on the foundations of the old nave.

A view of the Market Place, 1810, from Heginbotham. The original Market Charter was granted to the Lord of the Manor, Robert de Stokeport, around 1260 (see p. 7), although there is some evidence to suggest that a market may have been held prior to that date. The illustration shows the Shambles in front of the old church, while the shape of the Market Place is clearly recognizable.

A view of the Market Place, 1840, from an undated postcard published by M[ary] H. Twyford. A directory for 1910 describes her as a picture framer, at 9 Little Underbank. Notice the Bull's Head on the right and various shops, including Taylor's and Worthington's, and on the left, W.E. Leigh's shop and Victoria House. The early 1800s saw numerous changes in the Market Place, notably the removal of the Shambles.

This view from the rectory towards the parish church was photographed by the Revd Canon William Symonds early this century. He was inducted Rector of Stockport in 1875 and remained in office for forty-three years. He died on 15 March 1919, aged ninety-seven. His half brother, Revd Canon Arthur Symonds, was Rector of St Thomas's, Stockport, from 1886 to 1900.

By contrast, this view dates from around 1974. Among the shops, notice on the right Thatcher's bakers, established in the mid-1890s (see p. 6). Off to the right is the site of Loyalty Place, once the residence of 'Generous' John Lloyd, the magistrates' clerk at the time of the Luddite Riots in 1812. At that time the area was landscaped, with 'fountain, fishpond, shrub and tree'.

This undated commemorative postcard, produced by Reekie and Heaviside, is interesting but slightly inaccurate. John Wainwright was born at 58 Churchgate, Stockport, in 1723, and in 1747 was organist at the earlier parish church (see p. 9). In 1748 he moved to Manchester where he met John Byrom and composed the tune 'Stockport' (also known as 'Yorkshire', 'Huddersfield', etc!) to Byrom's words 'Christians Awake'. Wainwright became organist at Manchester Collegiate church (it did not achieve Cathedral status until 1847) in May 1767, when, to quote Heginbotham, the 'organist and singing man', Edward Betts, died. However, Wainwright himself died a few months later and was buried at Stockport on 23 January 1768.

This is a view of the Market Place from St Petersgate Bridge in Edwardian times, with the busy market, advertisements and street signs, those for Bennett's opticians, being very noticeable. Bennett's, established in 1823, was still in the town over a hundred years later. 'Life's greatest Gift is vision. Let optical science help you to preserve it': so read their advertisement in the 1933 issue of the [Stockport] Express Annual. Charles Elliott opened his butcher's shop at No. 18 Market Place (left), around 1900–1901. Note the Produce Hall, just left of centre.

The Produce Hall, also known as the Hen Market or Cheese Market, photographed around 1901, was built on the site of Stockport's first post office, vacated in 1836. The foundation stone of the single-storey market was laid in 1851, and the building was opened in 1852. The idea of providing the community with a free library was raised around 1853, but it was not until 1872 that the Council approved the provision of free libraries in the Borough. It was decided that the library would be housed above the Produce Hall and another storey was added. The library opened in 1875 and it remained here until the new Central Library was opened in 1913 (see p. 60). More recently the balcony's balustrade has been removed.

A 1911 advertisement for the Angel Inn when the proprietor was Cllr Peter Ridgway. The Angel off-licence, which sold Bell & Co.'s Fine Ales, and Helm's draper's shop flank the doorway. Various alterations to this very old building have exposed wattle and daub panels, timber framing and wooden beams. One licensee, James Crabbe, described in a local directory in 1820 as 'Dancing Master and High Constable', had earlier been billeted here as a bandsman with the Forfar Militia and had married the widowed landlady. The inn was the meeting place for the Philharmonic Society and local unions; concerts, dances and theatre performances took place here. Since the inn closed in 1951 the lower part of the building has been refronted.

In 1850 the Lord of the Manor of Stockport, Lord Vernon, sold the manorial rights to the Borough Council who began improvements. One of these was the construction, in 1861, of a covered market hall built of cast iron and glass, the lower sections of each side remained open and were enclosed later. We see here, in February 1969, a busy scene around the hall.

In June 1970 the 750th anniversary of the granting of the Borough Charter was celebrated. The week-long events opened on Saturday 20 June with a 'beating retreat' by the Mercian Volunteers in the Merseyway Precinct. Here, the Mayor, Alderman James Walton, is arriving at the parish church for the Civic Service on Sunday 21 June. Among the distinguished guests at the rear can be seen Councillor Harry Walker, Walter Knight (the leader of the Council) and Col. J.A. Christie-Miller (of the Christy hatting firm). Other events included a banquet, a schools' dance festival and concerts by the BBC Northern Symphony Orchestra, Stockport Youth Orchestra and the Fairey Band.

By the 1980s the hall was under threat of demolition due to its deteriorating condition, but it was refurbished, and reopened on 6 September 1985. Indoor stall holders are understandably in a celebratory mood in costumes reminiscent of earlier days.

Gresty's florists traded on the outdoor market for many years, but quite recently gave up their market stall to concentrate on their shops in Wellington Road South and Castle Street.

Mealhouse Brow, also known as Wynn Hill and Dungeon Brow, around 1901. The old town lockup is still in situ on the left hand side going down the hill to Lower Hillgate. Note the shops and their advertisements. There was Morris and Shaw who sold hams, bacon, cheese, etc. and served the town as provision merchants and cheese and bacon factors at 2 Mealhouse Brow from the late 1890s until around 1908 – the firm later became J.F. Shaw's and traded until the 1940s. J. Frank, advertising roller blinds, was at 9 Market Place from the late 1890s but had moved to Wellington Street by 1905. On the left is Boothby's, also cheese and bacon factors, who occupied various premises on Mealhouse Brow and at the corner of the Market Place from the 1870s until at least 1907.

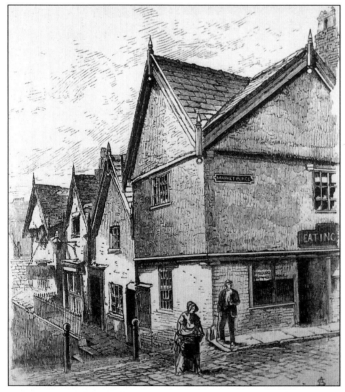

Rostron's Brow from an illustration from Heginbotham. This 'eating house' – Crossley's café – was dismantled in 1885 and re-erected in Vernon Park and converted into an aviary (see p. 73).

The Britannia Inn (second left), Churchgate, is believed to have dated from the 1790s. The earliest known licensee was Peter Turner in 1820. The inn was used as a meeting place by many early nineteenth-century reform organizations including the Chartists and the Anti-Corn Law League. An 1860 auction advertisement indicates that the inn had stables, a slaughterhouse and other outbuildings. Note the archway to gain access to the rear. The inn closed on 31 December 1953 and was later demolished; the site is now a car park.

Jim Hooley, a long-time member of the Stockport Historical Society, and the author of a pub guide and two local history trails, talking to members of the society on one of his popular local history walks in 1972. The Britannia Inn site is on the left, just off the picture – compare the unchanged roofline here with that of the buildings to the right of centre in the top picture.

In 1683 the Lord of the Manor, Edward de Warren of Poynton, built six one-roomed almshouses in 'The Folly' just behind the parish church as a thank-offering for the return of estates sequestrated during the Civil War. Intended for occupation by six old men, who each received an annuity of twenty shillings, the sole condition of tenancy was attendance at Divine Service – health permitting! The buildings passed into private ownership around 1884, when new almshouses were built in Turncroft Lane.

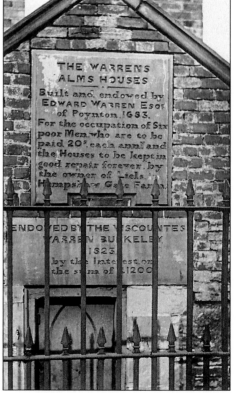

The Warren Almshouses became very dilapidated. On 10 October 1924 parts of three of them fell into Millgate and the row was demolished soon afterwards. These tablets, describing some of the history of the almshouses, have been preserved and can now be seen on the outside of the boundary wall of the parish church, above the grass banking at the east end.

A well-known Edwardian view of Bridge Street Brow, the steep hill up into the Market Place. The costumes of the children in the centre, and the lady on the right, indicate the period. The Boots chemist's shop on the right served the town from the turn of the century until the early 1970s; since then the building has housed a charity shop, a bread shop and a photographer's. The King's Arms public house on the left was also known as the Hole i'th'Wall. Since the 1970s its name has changed several times: The Castlewood gave way to a revival of the Hole i'th'Wall and it is now called Briarly's.

This view of Bridge Street looks towards the town across the old Lancashire Bridge. The location of Stockport's first, thirteenth-century, bridge is uncertain, but the River Mersey has been bridged at the foot of Bridge Street Brow (hence the road's name) since at least the seventeenth century. During the '45 rebellion the Royalist forces breached the bridge to halt the Jacobites' progress, although some did manage to enter the town by using the old ford. The Red Lion (right), 1 Prince's Street, dated from the 1780s and was a posting house for coaches. The earliest known licensee was Richard Owen in 1814.

There had been a public house on the site of the Warren Bulkeley Arms from at least the 1780s, although the earliest known licensee is William Higginson, 1816/17. In the nineteenth century this was the terminus for a horse-drawn omnibus service between Stockport and Manchester, as well as being the town's most fashionable inn, where banquets and balls were held. A meeting here, in March 1824, decided on the construction of the present Wellington Road, while one in November 1835 proposed the railway line from Stockport to Manchester. The Warren Bulkeley Arms, photographed in February 1970, was pulled down during the 1980s redevelopment scheme, but its 1890s frontage, shown here, was preserved and re-erected on Bridge Street as part of the Laura Ashley shop.

The view in this undated postcard in the 'Grenville Series' looks along Bridge Street in the direction of Lancashire Bridge and Tiviot Dale. The tram carries an advertisement for Gossage's. At the rear of the scene, on the right, is Watters tobacconist's (see p. 58). In the centre background, the white blind advertises Jackson's confectioners (Famous Sweets & Chocolates) which was here from the early 1890s to 1901/2. At the middle left is an advertisement for N. Gould & Co., The Stores, high class grocers/tea men, who were at 8 Bridge Street from the late 1890s, and at the right is T.W. Blackshaw's Café and Restaurant.

T. W. BLACKSHAW & SON

Caterers
—— AND ——
Refreshment Contractors

WEDDING BREAKFASTS, BALL SUPPERS, CINDERELLA DANCES, DINNERS, LUNCHEONS, GARDEN PARTIES, &c., Catered for in first-class style at reasonable prices.

MANUFACTURERS OF CHOCOLATES. :: ::
FIRST-CLASS CAFÉ & RESTAURANT. :: ::

All Orders are executed under own personal . supervision. .

TELEPHONE No. 175.

PLATE, CUTLERY, CHINA, GLASS, LINEN, and all requisites for Parties, &c., On Hire.

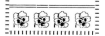

BRIDGE STREET,   ::   STOCKPORT.

This 1911 advertisement for T.W. Blackshaw speaks for itself!   -

Old Millgate, shown here in an illustration from Heginbotham, is possibly the route of the Roman road from Stockport to Melandra near Glossop. The name indicates that it was then the road to the (manorial) corn mill, which is known to have existed in 1457, but it may have dated from around 1270. A private commercial gas company, dating from 1820, bought land on Millgate in 1822 to establish its gasworks; this later became the site for Stockport Corporation's electricity generating station (see p. 84).

The County Hotel, 13 Millgate, was erected around 1895 on the site of one of the various 'Pack Horse' public houses, whose first recorded licensee was Nathaniel Fox in 1824. The hotel was demolished as part of the Asda supermarket development scheme.

In the late seventeenth century the Warren family, Lords of the Manor of Stockport, purchased Millgate Hall, a timber-framed building, as their town house. In 1732, and again later, brick wings were added. William Sykes of Edgeley opened a handloom weaving factory in the building in 1804, and by 1814 power-looms had taken over.

The upper photograph shows the exterior view, while this lower photograph shows more clearly the sad condition into which the building had fallen. Here we see part of a decorative plasterwork frieze probably dating from the seventeenth century. This photograph was taken not long before the Hall was demolished in 1927.

The original Park Silk Mill dated from 1732 and is the earliest known water-powered factory not only in Stockport but also in the north west. It was later replaced by cotton mills owned at various times by (Sir) Ralph Pendlebury (in 1810) and the Marsland family, who also had a bleach works here. The mills saw various stages of building and rebuilding, as well as a boiler explosion in 1851 in which twenty-two lives were lost.

F.S. Johnson Ltd, cotton doublers, Melville Street, occupied Park Mills from 1897 until 1954. The premises were eventually demolished around 1984; the site is now occupied by Sainsbury's which was built on the mill's foundations which are still visible from the opposite side of the river. The Johnson family home was 'The Paddocks' in Davenport (see p. 122).

Two

The Hillgates and the Underbanks

A view down Lower Hillgate dating from around 1970. Note Quayle's shop (middle right) which still bears a date stone of 1897, when George Quayle was the proprietor. He sold hosiery and gloves but specialized in shirts. The Quayle family (see also p. 31) traded at various addresses in the town from the 1890s to the 1970s. The shop is still (in July 1998) a clothes shop. Nearer the camera, Mellor's (right) is now Prontaprint, and the next building up the street is the Gladstone Arms, formerly the Bishop Blaize. Named in honour of the Patron Saint of Woolworkers, certainly from the 1820s, it seems to have changed its name to the Gladstone Arms with the tenancy of Joseph Tolson, around 1872, and has recently reverted to its original name. On 15 June 1852 a Royal Proclamation reminded Catholics of earlier laws forbidding any display of Roman Catholic ceremony or worship, except privately or in a Catholic Church. In spite of this, Catholic priests exercised 'their rites and ceremonies ... in highways and places of public resort ... to the manifest danger of public peace ... during the time of [Anglican] Divine Service, and in such a manner as to disturb the congregation assembled therein'. On Sunday 27 June 1852 some two thousand of Stockport's Roman Catholics participated in their 'annual procession' apparently in defiance of the order. This caused strong feelings in the community and on the following Tuesday there was an argument between Catholics and Protestants in the Bishop Blaize. This escalated into a full-scale riot: Catholics destroyed Protestants' property, and Protestants, in retaliation, wrecked St Michael's Mission Chapel and the Church of St Philip and St James.

There has been a White Lion pub on this site since at least the seventeenth century and probably earlier. John Byng (Lord Torrington) stayed here in 1790, describing it in his diary as 'sad-looking' and very heavily timbered. He paid 7d for breakfast and 10d for a good supper, being served by a black waiter, 'a quick and intelligent fellow'. The White Lion was remodelled in the 1830s, and rebuilt altogether in 1904. Here, the new building is being erected behind the existing one, which was then demolished. At the left is the shop occupied, from the mid-1870s until 1905, by Adamson's tailors; this was later Diane's dress shop and is now the Yorkshire Building Society.

Union Road, from an undated postcard, but after 1904 as the new White Lion is at the left, as we look towards Little Underbank and St Petersgate Bridge. Opened in 1868 this bridge was the gift of the Wright family of Offerton (see p. 54) and gave the first level access to the Market Place – all other approaches being either uphill or downhill.

The White Lion can clearly be identified in this photograph, dated between 1911 and 1914. The Motor Cycle Club was based at the Mersey Hotel (see p. 43) until 1911 when it transferred to the White Lion.

John Nield & Son purchased James Turner & Son's piano and music seller's business around 1880. James Turner had started in 1859. Nield died in 1890 and his son Robert H. Nield took over. Robert later covered the yard to enlarge the business, which adjoined Underbank Hall. By 1911 he advertised his shop as 'The Biggest Piano Showroom in the North of England'; and this photograph dates from around that time. He died in 1920 but the business continued, eventually becoming a partnership with Hardy's pianos in the mid-1950s. (Hardy's had started at Lancashire Hill in the early 1880s). The site is now occupied by modern offices.

A policeman and postman figure prominently in this picture of part of Pickford's Brow around 1901 but almost certainly they were stuck on afterwards by the photographer to create some foreground interest! The background repays closer study. Note the tightly packed housing, and the advertisements on the gable end: Pears' Soap – 'You Dirty Boy'; Goodall's Egg Powder and Custard Powder; Goodall's Gravy Browning at 6d a bottle, but not *this* size!; and Pitts's Furnishings at Gaythorn, Manchester.

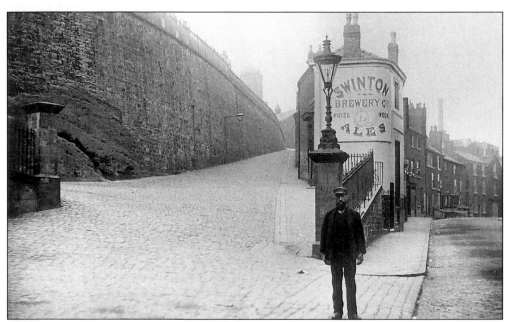

Looking towards High Bankside (see p. 54) around 1901, with St Peter's Church dome just visible at the top of the rise. The Swinton Brewery's pub was the White Hart (now long since demolished). The row of houses has now been replaced by a row of single-storey shops.

A closer look at the White Hart on Chestergate, showing Mrs Gladys Stuart, the licensee's wife, in 1908, shortly before she died. Her husband, George, held the licence until the pub closed in 1913. Note that the brewery was, by now, Watson & Woodhead. The advertisements on the windows are for Haig's Glenleven Whisky and Martell's Three Star Brandy. The end wall panel indicates the award of a medal at the Brewers' Exhibition, London.

In 1938, with war threatening, it was decided that Stockport should be provided with deep, bombproof air raid shelters. Begun in October that year, with the aid of a Government grant, the tunnels lie beneath 30ft of sandstone rock. It took 30 men with pneumatic drills 12 months to excavate them. There were 6 entrances including one in Royal Oak Yard. The tunnels extend for almost a mile; there are 2 main passages with 19 cross-passages, all 7ft high and 7ft wide. Wooden forms and electric lighting were provided, together with a first aid post, canteen and toilets (of a kind!). The Chestergate shelters accommodated some 4,000 people; similar shelters were provided at Portwood (3,000), Old Road, Heaton Norris (2,000), Brinksway (4,000) and Stewart Street (2,000). Opened in wartime, October 1939, the Chestergate shelters are now a first class tourist attraction.

Underbank Hall, one of Stockport's best known buildings, was the former town house of the Ardernes of Harden Hall, Bredbury, and dates from at least the sixteenth century. It was sold by auction in 1823. Some of the townspeople hoped to acquire it as a town hall, but four gentlemen – William Miller Christy, John Kenyon Winterbottom, John Worsley and Isaac Lloyd – bought the hall for 3,000 guineas. In December 1824 they announced their intention to open the building as a bank – it is still a bank, now the NatWest. Only the frontage, some of the front rooms, attics and entrance hall remain from those early days. The rear of the building, extended in the eighteenth century, was pulled down in 1916 to make room for the present banking hall. Fortunately, the ancient fireplace (brought here from Utkinton Hall, Cheshire, in 1623 as part of the dowry of Eleanor Done, who married Ralph Arderne) was preserved and can still be seen.

This view of the Three Shires (centre), a timber-framed building (possibly sixteenth-century) of a similar style to Underbank Hall, was taken around 1901. It was built on land belonging to the Legh family of Adlington Hall and may have been part of their town house. It was sold in the 1820s and part of it was purchased for use as solicitors' offices, a function it retains to this day. The remainder of the original building has been used variously as a shop and a café and is now the Three Shires wine bar. To the left is Charles Septimus Hudson's shop at 34 Great Underbank. He advertises BSA fittings, Miller's famous cycle lamps and Elsbach incandescent lights. The shop was demolished in the late 1960s. Correspondents recall a brush works, behind Hudson's shop, approached through the archway.

A photograph of Quayle's Beehive taken just after it closed in 1978. The Beehive was run by various members of the Johnson family from the early 1880s until around 1905/6, when William Quayle took over. The shop supplied shirts and underwear for the local police until its closure. Since Quayle's left, the building has housed a restaurant, a chip shop, a general goods store and a greengrocer's; it is now the Country Garden sandwich shop and restaurant, with no trace of the old Beehive sign.

THE LEADING HOUSE IN THE DISTRICT

—FOR—

Ladies'	Gent.'s
Dress	Shirts,
Goods,	Collars,
Dress	Ties,
Trimmings,	Gloves,
Laces,	Hose,
Insertions,	Pyjama
Silks,	Suits,
Velvets,	Nightshirts,
Blouses,	Fancy
Fancy	Waistcoats,
Neckwear,	Umbrellas,
Skirts,	Caps,
Corsets,	Unshrinkable
Haberdashery.	Underwear.

W. L. QUAYLE, BEEHIVE, UNDERBANK, and 43 St. Petersgate, Stockport

This advertisement is from 1911.

By 1910 the Maypole Dairy Co. had branches at 15 Lower Hillgate and at 63 Castle Street, Edgeley. This undated photograph shows the staff at the Lower Hillgate branch. Note those prices!

A view of Lower Hillgate, taken from an Edwardian postcard. The chemist and druggist's shop (left) was occupied by Kay's from around 1878. It was taken over by J.C. Arnfield (see p. 47), a former Kay's employee, around 1887. The half-timbered building, at 11-13 Lower Hillgate, was remodelled for Chatterton's in 1888 and was still occupied by them in the 1960s; it is now the home of the Scripture Union. At the right, at 8 and 10, is Redman's, famous for its dried fruits and nuts, among other things.

This is Middle Hillgate, early this century. In the mid-1970s, after White's had ceased trading, many of the fitments were acquired by Stockport Museum where they are now displayed. Just beyond this shop is 'the big lamp' (see cover) which is over the entrance to The (Higher) Pack Horse public house, recently re-opened as The Lamp and extended into the former White's shop. Beyond the lamp is the Salvation Army Citadel founded in 1894, the 'Sally Army' having come to Stockport in 1882. The Salvation Army's architect was W. Gilbee Scott of London. The site had originally been intended for use as a police station to serve the Hillgate area.

In 1920 the Salvation Army purchased the Hatters' Arms, also known as the Rag and Louse (closed in 1913) which was adjacent to the Citadel. They demolished it and erected the Young People's Hall. The foundation stone was laid on 20 March 1920 and the completed hall, built by local builder Daniel Eadie, was opened by Councillor John Greenhalgh in 1922. The photograph of this event is endorsed on the back: 'This is the opening of the New Hall. Lucy'.

Joseph Blackshaw was one of a family of bakers who served the town from at least the 1870s. As a Borough Councillor he was one of the ten dignitaries who each laid a foundation stone for the Salvation Army Citadel in 1894. He died on 20 January 1924, aged seventy-one. Blackshaw's ceased trading in the 1970s; the shop was demolished but the frontage is preserved in Stockport Museum. The site of the shop is now a car park.

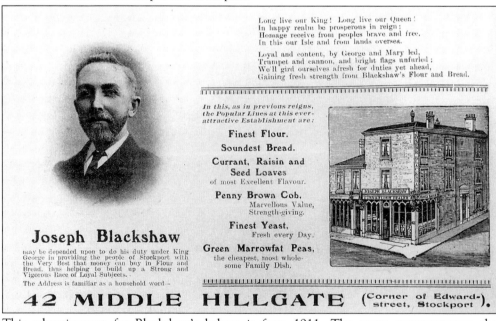

This advertisement for Blackshaw's bakery is from 1911. The verse commemorates the coronation of King George V and Queen Mary. The shop was famous for its quality goods – the recipe for currant bread was supposedly secret. Older Stockport residents have reported that you could even buy half a loaf if you couldn't afford a whole one!

With Blackshaw's in the background, this view shows the building occupied by Smethurst's Heating and Ventilation Co. Ltd. It is the former Old Admiral public house (38 Middle Hillgate) believed to date from the 1820s, although the first recorded licensee was James Williamson in 1831 and this is the date which appeared on a downspout at the back. The pub closed on 31 December 1959 and was then let to other businesses. The archway led to the 'New Market', erected after the Court Leet suggested, in 1835, that more market space was needed. It was then discovered that this new vegetable and potato market was illegal, as it infringed the rights of the Lord of the Manor. Following demolition in 1979, this area was converted into a small car park.

Situated at the corner of Middle Hillgate and Waterloo Road, next to the Black Lion pub, the original Tabernacle (1702) was the first Dissenters' chapel to be erected in the town under the Toleration Act (1689). It was built for Richard Milne, its first minister, who retired in 1718. Solomon Ashton, the minister 1804–1806, was so popular that the chapel was always crowded. It was rebuilt in 1807. There was a small cemetery at the front, later paved over, and another at the rear which later had the chapel's school built over it. After the chapel closed it was occupied as business premises and was then taken over as Sergeant Pepper's Club. In 1975 fire damaged the building beyond repair and it was demolished in 1979. The foundations and the graveyards now lie under grass and shrubs.

This photograph of the Grapes Steps cottages (long since demolished) at Covent Garden, Middle Hillgate can be dated by a poster advertising the sale of tools by auction on Thursday 18 September 1890. Other posters advertise rail travel, Armour's extract of beef, Amies for Boots (they had premises at 32 Little Underbank, and at 40–2 Castle Street, Edgeley, in 1910), and a Stockport *v.* Wrexham football match. In the background can be seen the Hen and Chickens public house.

Hillgate House, 27 Higher Hillgate (left), was built in 1742 by Mr Chadwick, then bought by Samuel Oldknow in 1785. Oldknow built an adjoining mill where he installed Stockport's first steam engine in 1791. In 1801/2 the property was let to William Radcliffe, inventor of the dressing-frame which made power-loom weaving practicable. In 1822 the *Stockport Advertiser* was founded here by Mr James Lomax. In 1836 the house was rented by Christy's (famous for towels and hats), and was then bought by them in 1846. After Mr Wakefield Christy became the tenant of Bramall Hall in 1860, Hillgate House was used as offices, though occasionally family members stayed there. Colonel J.A. Christie-Miller recalled that they still had to use an old tin bath as late as the 1940s! Following the demise of the business, in 1997, the Hillgate House premises were vacated and put up for sale. By the 1980s the houses adjoining Hillgate House had been replaced by a modern industrial unit.

Here we see male hatters and female hat trimmers backed by the banner which celebrated the setting up of the women's union alongside the men's in 1888. The banner bears a large version of their union label which was devised in 1893. In 1907 all the Stockport hat firms became unionized for the first time and this photograph may reflect that notable victory.

This advertisement from 1911 shows a patented hat ventilation system. The Hat Manufacturers' Supply Co. Ltd, Pretoria Works, is listed in a directory for 1910 as a 'hat-tip printers' in Chestergate.

Stockport Sunday School, from an undated postcard 'printed in Germany', but it must date from after 1909 as it shows Centenary Hall at the right of the main building. The first local Sunday School, a joint venture between the Anglicans, Methodists and Nonconformists, began in 1784. In 1794 the Methodists decided to have their own independent interdenominational school. By 1803 there were over 200 teachers and almost 3,000 pupils, and to accommodate this growth new premises, erected off Lower Hillgate, were opened in 1806. This became the largest Sunday school in the world. Four storeys high, it had fifty-eight classrooms and a further wing was added in 1835/6.

Stockport Sunday School ladies' procession, part of the 106th Anniversary Annual Procession on Sunday 18 June 1911. The local press reported that, in spite of damp weather, 2,888 teachers, pupils and officials took part. The route from the Sunday School was along Wellington Street and Wellington Road South to Longshut Lane, turning back along Wellington Road South to St Petersgate, ending in the Market Place.

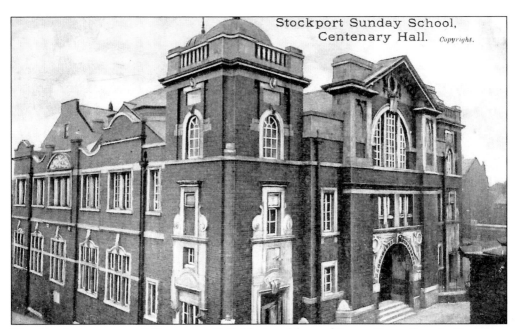

Stockport Sunday School, Centenary Hall. *Copyright.*

The foundation stone of Centenary Hall (designed by architects, Potts, Son & Hennings, Manchester) was laid on 5 October 1907 by the Mayoress, Mrs Henry Bell. The building was opened by Lady Sheffield on 9 October 1909. The Sunday School and Centenary Hall were demolished in 1971, as the town had turned down Councillor Harry Walker's suggestion that Centenary Hall might be used as a much needed Arts Centre.

A view of the Centenary Hall's main hall in 1971, not long before the building was demolished. The hall measured 74ft by 58ft at ground level, and was 115ft long at gallery level; it seated 2,200 people. The organ, installed later, was the gift of members of the Leigh family in memory of the late James Leigh, general manager of the school for a number of years.

In 1759 Edmund Watson sold a plot of land in the Carrs to Willoughby Ashbrook and John Cooper, giving them permission to build a silk mill, dam and wheel. This became Stockport's second water powered silk mill (see p. 24) and formed the nucleus of a very important industrial area. After some changes of ownership, Charles Davis bought the concern in 1781, converting and rebuilding the mill for cotton spinning. The rebuilt mill consisted of two six-storey factories each measuring 25yds long by 8yds wide. In 1789 Samuel Oldknow began spinning his own yarn here. By 1828 three-quarters of the town's cotton waste spinners were based here in the Carrs, and in 1836 half of the town's candlewick manufacturers were also based here.

The source of the water was the Tin (or Hempshaw) Brook, highlighted in this photograph of the Carrs under snow, taken in March 1969. Just after 10 a.m. on Sunday 4 June 1967, an Argonaut DC4 aircraft belonging to Midland Airways crashed in Hopes Carr on its approach to Manchester Airport (then Ringway). Only twelve of the eighty-four people on board survived. A memorial has recently been placed at the site.

Orchard Street Chapel was described by Heginbotham as being 'pleasantly situated' in the middle of a field through which a footpath (now Waterloo Road) ran between Hillgate and Churchgate. Built in 1788 and remodelled in the 1850s, it was a Congregational Chapel until 1866, when the congregation moved to their new chapel on Wellington Road South. From 1866 the building served as a working men's club for Henry Faulder's (see p. 83). It later became Orchard Street Mission Chapel (1891–1902) then just 'a chapel' until 1907, since when it has been occupied as business premises and considerably refurbished in recent years.

Orchard Street Sunday School was founded by the Revd Absalom Clark around 1860, during his ministry which began in 1847. The building was later occupied as business premises. It has now given way to modern offices built in a sympathetic style. The name 'Orchard Street' is possibly derived from the name of land shown bordering 'Croft' and 'Parson's Middle Orchard' on a map dated 1577. Both these photographs date from May 1974.

41

Formerly known as the Sir Sydney Smith, this building, first noted in 1809, stood at the corner of Waterloo Road and Spring Gardens and was later renamed The Grapes. The first recorded licensee was James Pickford in 1821. A remodelled road junction now covers the area.

Three

Mersey Square and the Precinct

Stockport's first Fire Brigade HQ was in Corporation Street. Volunteer firemen were called to fires by the ringing of a bell in the parish church tower. The Central Fire Station (left) was a very handsome building with provision for six engines and was opened on 10 April 1902. It is understood that its distinctive tower, on the left in this early postcard, was sometimes used for scaling practice. Sadly the building was demolished in 1967. The Tramway Offices and sheds are visible just to the right of the fire station. Electric tramways began in 1901 with routes from Mersey Square to Sandy Lane, Woodley station and the Robin Hood Hotel in Brinksway, with further routes in 1903. The Council bought the Stockport and Hazel Grove Carriage and Tramway Company in 1904, electrifying its routes in 1905. At the time of this view the River Mersey, the old boundary between Lancashire and Cheshire, was still visible through the town centre. It was not culverted until the late 1930s prior to the first Merseyway opening in 1940 (see p. 47). The Mersey Hotel (far right) was formerly the Mersey Inn, its first recorded licensee being Abraham Unsworth from at least 1838 until the 1850s. In 1863 the pub was described in a local sale notice as having its own six-barrel brewery, as well as being the meeting place for four local clubs.

This 'Grenville Series, Stockport' postcard is impressed with the postmark '28 August 1913'. The tram carries an advertisement for Crawford's Cream Crackers, the Mersey Hotel is styled as 'commercial' and the advertisements for Hidderley's (at the top of the hill) and Harry Garner, sign writer (on the left going up the hill) are quite visible.

This shows the traffic chaos in Mersey Square in the early 1960s – certainly before 1967 as the fire station (centre) is still prominent. Except for one bus operated by Manchester Corporation (route No. 74), those with dark coloured roofs belong to the North Western Road Car Company Ltd; the others were operated by Stockport Corporation Transport Department. The spire of Christ Church, Heaton Norris, is visible in the background.

Accounts of the accident which killed Superintendent Howard Beckwith vary in detail. One account says that the *Mary Dalziel* (fire engines had names in those days), a Belsize fire engine built in 1910, left the fire station and went straight ahead by the side of what became known as 'the Bear Pit', with the intention of turning left up Wellington Road South. It is thought to have skidded and failed to make the turn, continuing straight ahead and through the retaining wall. Another version has it that it went across Mersey Square (there were no traffic islands then), turned left into Wellington Road South, travelled a short distance then crashed through the stone wall of Wellington Bridge to drop 40ft into New Bridge, now Chestergate, below. It was responding to an emergency call received at 4.12 a.m. on 29 December 1926 reporting a fire at the offices of solicitor Henry Jackson, Halifax Buildings, Wellington Street. The driver was Assistant Superintendent John Rushby, who was severely injured, as was Fireman George Rogers; both were trapped. Superintendent Beckwith, a former master mariner, was pronounced dead on arrival at Stockport Infirmary. As a young man he had sailed on clipper ships, including the famous *Cutty Sark*. He joined the Stockport fire service from Bootle in 1897 and among many awards received the King's Police and Fire Brigade Medal in the New Year's honours list in 1926. He was sixty-four years old when he died. The photograph shows Supt. Beckwith's funeral cortege on Wellington Road, looking south towards the Town Hall, on New Year's Day 1927. His coffin was carried on the fire engine *James Fernley*, driven by Sergeant J.F. Dawson; it was draped with the Union Jack and the Superintendent's helmet, belt and axe were on top. He is buried in the Borough Cemetery. A memorial tablet to him, on the front wall of the Central Fire Station, was unveiled in 1929. This tablet was re-sited on the wall leading down to Mersey Square bus station from Wellington Bridge after the fire station was demolished.

This photograph, taken in the yard of the Central Fire Station, shows the wrecked *Mary Dalziel*. Standing at the back is Fireman Harold Ryder, who later became Chief Fire Officer (1948–1962). Left to right, front row: Superintendent John Rushby, Assistant Superintendent J.F. Dawson, -?-, Fireman F. James, Fireman W. 'Bill' Ratcliffe, Sgt G. Capper. Messrs Rushby and Dawson were promoted on 11 March 1927, and Sgt Capper became Assistant Superintendent in 1928. Mr Rushby and Mr Capper both retired in March 1942.

The Dennis Motor Pump, registration number DB 7961, was purchased in 1927 to replace the *Mary Dalziel*. It is described as 'No. 1 fire engine' and was equipped with a 35ft wooden extension ladder, a turbine pump and a 40 gallon water tank. The motorcycle in the background has the registration number NU 9525.

The first Merseyway dated from 1940, (see p. 43). However, in the 1960s a plan for the wholesale redevelopment of the main shopping areas was drawn up. This 'intermediate' photograph was taken just prior to the clearance of the town centre for the new precinct in 1967. Note the new flats being built on the hill at Heaton Norris (left); also visible are St Mary's Roman Catholic Church and Pendlebury Hall.

Further along the road to the right from the previous view are the frontages of Marks & Spencer's, Woolworth's and British Home Stores. Behind the latter can be seen the premises of J.C. Arnfield, an old established pharmaceutical chemists (see p. 32). Although the company merged with James Woolley Sons & Co. Ltd, the Manchester wholesale druggists and manufacturing chemists, in 1936 (five years after Mr Arnfield's death) the firm retained its separate identity, trading here until the 1960s. Also to be seen are the supports upon which the original Merseyway was built.

The section of Heaton Lane between Tiviot Dale and Mersey Square was renamed Prince's Street in honour of the visit of the Prince and Princess of Wales to open the Town Hall on 7 July 1908 (see pp. 65–8), and this postcard dates to before that time. Note the period costume, as well as the premises of Wallace's bootmakers (left), who traded from around 1904 until the 1920s, and Booth's tobacconists (right), who moved here from Shaw Heath around 1900/1901 and had left by 1906. Carrington's grocer's (right background), who began trading around 1880, was still here in 1939.

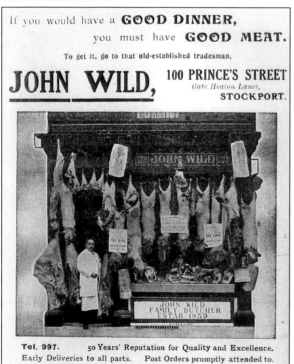

If you would have a **GOOD DINNER,** you must have **GOOD MEAT.**

To get it, go to that old-established tradesman,

JOHN WILD, 100 PRINCE'S STREET *(late Heaton Lane),* STOCKPORT.

Tel. 997.   50 Years' Reputation for Quality and Excellence.
Early Deliveries to all parts.   Post Orders promptly attended to.

Prime Cheshire Veal Kidneys, Corned Beef and Tongues always on hand.

This 1911 advertisement for a local butcher confirms the change of name from Heaton Lane to Prince's Street. The shop front indicates that the business, which appears in local directories from 1887 until the 1920s, was established in 1859.

Next door to John Wild, at 102 Prince's Street, was William Harvey's saddler and harness maker's shop. His business was established in Heaton Lane/Prince's Street around 1883, with later additional premises in Port Street. He came to Stockport from Shrewsbury as a boy. President of the Lancashire Saddlers Association, and one-time President of the National Association, he traded for over fifty years and after his death, in 1936, the family continued in business until the mid-1960s. During the First World War he was an Inspector with the town's Special Constables, and was awarded the MBE for his services.

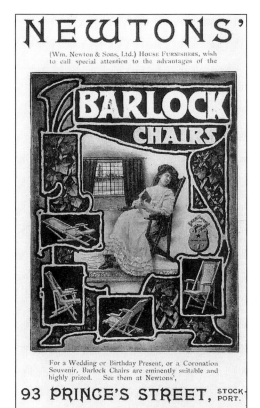

Across Prince's Street from Harvey's and Wild's was William Newton's house furnisher's shop. He started the business in Edgeley in the late 1880s, moving to Heaton Lane/Prince's Street around 1888. He has an interesting suggestion for Coronation souvenirs!

49

The Touchstone public house stood at the corner of Prince's Street and Wellington Road North, where Debenhams' store now stands. The licensee in 1849 was Elizabeth Bowers but the pub was much older: an advertisement in 1857 offers 'to be let, that old-established beerhouse known as 'The Touchstone' ... with brewhouse ... suitable for doing a first-rate business. The city omnibuses pass and re-pass every half-hour in the day'. A 'newly-built' Touchstone was licensed to Samuel Shepley in 1859/60. The most likely reason for the pub's name is that it commemorates a racehorse which won the St Leger in 1834, ridden by G. Calloway. (The Flying Dutchman on Hillgate was also named after a racehorse). The Touchstone closed on 25 February 1974.

This Talbot Garage advertisement dates from 1911. A 1910 directory lists the proprietor as Mr R.B. Emerson. A 1924 directory lists Charles Stafford as the proprietor; he is also listed as 'Charles Stafford Ltd, Ford service dealers'. It is understood that he was a former butcher who used to live in Love Lane but who later lived at 'Ravenscroft', St Lesmo Road, Edgeley, a large house in its own grounds.

50

Stockport was first lit by gas in December 1821. The gasworks in Millgate and Heaton Lane were purchased by the Council from the Stockport Gas Company in 1838 for £21,493. Additional works were opened at Portwood in 1878, with the Millgate works closing in 1895 and the Heaton Lane works (seen here) in 1930. Note the public weighing machine (right foreground). The Cotton Tree Hotel was licensed to Daniel Adamson in 1820. Following tenancy changes, John Cocker took on the licence in August 1865, advertising that he intended 'to conduct the business in the same upright and straightforward manner' as his predecessor, selling 'the purest and most wholesome beverages at reasonable prices'. In September he was advertising 'Come and dine at Cocker's Cotton Tree Inn. Every Friday at One'. The name board offers 'Groves & Whitnall's Ales & Crown Stout & Wines', while an advertisement on the wall offers 'Good Accommodation for Cyclists' and 'Stabling'. The pub closed in March 1920.

Built on the site of the Heaton Lane Gasworks, the new tramway/bus depot was opened by Councillor T.E. Hunt on 28 July 1932. Unused for a time in the late 1970s, part of it was utilized for Youth Training Scheme accommodation. It was demolished in 1982 and the site, adjoining the Heaton Lane multi-storey car park, is at present being redeveloped as offices.

Designed by G.W. Buck, the Manchester & Birmingham Railway's chief engineer, and built by Tomkinson and Holmes of Liverpool, the first Stockport viaduct was begun early in 1839 and was completed in December 1840. The foundations rest in bedrock with excavations from 6ft to 20ft deep. The viaduct is one-third of a mile long, has 27 arches and stands 106ft above the river. Opened to passenger traffic in 1842, it had only 2 tracks and soon became a bottleneck, with 250 passenger trains and 140 goods trains crossing it each day. The London & North Western Railway planned to widen the viaduct by building in cast iron, but the Council insisted that they should use brick. The extension was built 1887–90. The factory at the right, with its white lettering, is the premises of Charles Crossley & Son on Astley Street.

(WILLIAM CROSSLEY.)

ESTABLISHED 50 YEARS.

Heaton Norris Tin Works.

Charles Crossley & Son,

IRON, ZINC, and
TINPLATE WORKERS,

MAKERS OF ALL KINDS OF SHEET METAL WORK
FOR MANUFACTURERS, MACHINISTS, Etc.

OUR ONLY ADDRESS :

Astley Street, Heaton Lane

(NEAR RAILWAY ARCHES),

STOCKPORT.

Tele. No. 958.   *Residence—3 Lowfield Grove.*

Although there was a W.H. Crossley's Sheet Metal Works in Edgeley, established around 1820, Charles Crossley & Son seem to have started around 1861; this advertisement from 1911 says 'established 50 years'. The business first occupied premises off Heaton Lane/Prince's Street, moving to Astley Street in the mid-1880s. It is still there, trading under the same name, carrying on the same business and William Crossley's great-grandson works there! William, a Rechabite and a staunch supporter of Stockport Sunday School, worked until he was ninety-two! He died, aged ninety-eight, in January 1952.

Four

St Peter's Square and St Petersgate

St. Peter's Square, Stockport

The town's first Theatre Royal began in the old Temperance Hall. Its own permanent premises opened in 1874 but were burned down in 1887. It was rebuilt as the Theatre Royal and Opera House in 1888. Although used for the town's first cinema performance in June 1896, it retained its theatre status until January 1957 when it closed after the Christmas season's pantomime, *The Old Woman who lived in a Shoe*. After standing empty for five years, it was sold for £27,000, then demolished. The site then became a Fine Fare supermarket which closed in 1971; the building has since been a do-it-yourself store, a Co-operative Bank and an Abbey National Building Society. It is at present 'To Let'. This postcard view must date from after 1901 as it shows the wires for the electric trams.

In 1890 a tramway service similar to the one seen here, with St Peter's Church in the background, began operating between St Peter's Square and the Bull's Head, Hazel Grove. The first electric tram service to Hazel Grove began in July 1905. St Peter's Church dates from 1768 and was built at the expense of William Wright of Offerton (see p. 57) whose monument it contains; the chancel was added in 1888.

This is from a coloured postcard of High Bankside and Pickford's Brow, 'published at No. 9 Little Underbank, Stockport'. It was sent on 22 December 1908 to 'Dear John' in Canada, 'with love from Elsie' at 27 Berlin Road, Edgeley, to thank him 'for the beautiful broace' [sic]. Note the steps at the left – there is still a flight of steps here, but the tightly packed housing has gone.

Founded in 1844, St Peter's National School, situated next to the church, opened in 1845. Extended in 1872, it was used from the 1880s as both a day and Sunday school. It is seen here, just prior to demolition, in the early 1970s. The site has now been landscaped with a footpath leading from St Peter's Square to the Rock Craft Centre.

Latterly occupied by Green & Moult, solicitors, this mid-eighteenth-century building was formerly Alderman Graham's house, which was attacked by Roman Catholic rioters in 1852 (see p. 25), probably because he was known as a staunch Protestant. The house was a listed building and was the subject of a public enquiry before consent to demolish was given. At the demolition, in 1977, the roof slates and doorcase were removed for reuse elsewhere; unfortunately the handrail and steps, also earmarked for reuse, were destroyed when the front wall collapsed on them.

Further along St Peter's Square from Green & Moult's was Central Buildings and Hidderley's wallpaper shop; this whole area is now occupied by 1 St Peter's Square. Hidderley's, still remembered by many residents, traded in the town from the mid-1870s. The photograph, from the late 1960s or early 1970s, also shows the Trimming Shop and the Corset Shop, and an advertisement for Universal Checks, motor insurance and personal finance, above the arched pediment.

Initial construction of the Prudential Buildings in St Petersgate was interrupted by the First World War. The buildings were opened on 28 September 1922 by the Mayor, Alderman Charles Royle JP. Faced in Darley Dale stone, they were designed by the firm's architect, Paul Waterhouse who was, at that time, President of the Royal Institute of British Architects. The caterers for the occasion were T.W. Blackshaw & Sons (see p. 21). The building is now solicitors' offices and a restaurant. Note the queue for the Theatre Royal (see p. 53). This undated postcard is probably from the late 1920s.

This 'Grenville series' postcard published
at No. 14 St Peter's Square is postmarked
'Stockport July 16 1909', and was sent to
'Dear Bertha' (Mrs Astington) at Southport
with 'Love from Laura & family'. The
Empire Theatre, built on the site of the
Grand Theatre (demolished 1904), was
renamed the Hippodrome in 1915. It was
a cinema (1931–40) and a theatre again
(1940–51), then the Astor Cinema until
it was burned out on 5 March 1960; it was
demolished in 1965.

The Mansion House in High Street was
built by William Wright of Offerton as
his chief residence. Heginbotham reports
that it was already the headquarters of the
Stockport Conservative Association by
1892. When the building was demolished
in the early 1970s, the Conservatives
moved to the New Mansion House on
Wellington Road South and the site
of the old Mansion House became the
Employment Exchange and car park.

In business since 1866, Peter Watters had tobacconists' shops at Heaton Lane and Greek Street by the early 1890s. By 1902 he had additional shops at Tiviot Dale and in St Petersgate (above). In 1905 the former was managed by Mrs Fields and the latter by A. Westbrook, who became his partner. The firm of Watters & Westbrook appears in directories from 1906. Arthur Westbrook died on a voyage from Buenos Aires in April 1926. Peter Watters died in October 1931, aged eighty-four. This branch continued trading – the photograph was taken in April 1970 – until the shop was demolished for road widening in the late 1970s. The shop with the oriel window (recently occupied by Abbatt Toys) still remains. Note the former Ritz Cinema in the background.

An advertisement from 1933.

Five

Wellington Road South and the Town Hall

This aerial view is from an undated, but probably 1930s, postcard 'Sold only by E. Wright, Newsagent, Stockport'. The main buildings, viewed from the bottom to the top of the picture are, on the right: the Super Cinema (built 1910 and closed in 1965), the coalyards, the Infirmary and the War Memorial Art Gallery. On the left are the Central Library and the Town Hall.

Stockport's first Mechanics' Institute only lasted from 1825 to 1827. Its successor, 'The Stockport Institution for the Diffusion of Useful Knowledge' began meeting in an old theatre in Park Street in 1834, later leasing premises in Lower Hillgate. The directors then resolved to erect their own premises and bought land at the corner of St Petersgate and Wellington Road South. The foundation stone was laid by James Kershaw MP, on 8 June 1861 and the building, shown here in an illustration from Heginbotham was opened by Lord Stanley on 22 September 1862. The Great Hall seated 1,000 people and there was a library of several thousand volumes. The building was replaced in 1912–13 by the Central Library, as the small Free Library in the Market Place (see p. 13) was by now totally inadequate for the town's expanding population. The philanthropist Andrew Carnegie contributed £15,000 towards the cost of the new Central Library.

This 'Grenville Series' postcard predates 1913, as the Mechanics' Institute is visible at the left. Across the road is the entrance to the railway station, while the Town Hall with its distinctive tower can be seen to the right of centre.

This Bullock Bros postcard is postmarked 'Stockport, August 27 1903'. Addressed to Miss Bertha Hooley, c/o Miss Whittaker at Blackpool, part of the message reads: 'What do you think of Tom Potts' wedding on the other side?'. This helps us to date the picture exactly. Tom Potts, aged twenty-six, a journeyman hatter of Lowfield Road, married Edith Hopkinson, aged twenty-two, daughter of a foreman hatter, of Adswood Lane East, at Mount Tabor Church, Wellington Road South, on Monday 1 June 1903. The local press reported 'for some time before the wedding party arrived, a large number of people assembled at the chapel ...'. The photograph shows the chapel (far left), with onlookers to the wedding, the National School and the Congregational Church (in the centre); the Technical School is opposite.

This 'Grenville Series' postcard, postmarked 'Stockport, 12 August, 1938' has a cancellation mark advertising the Empire Exhibition at Glasgow, May–October 1938. Stockport's first Methodist New Connexion Mount Tabor Chapel was in London Square (1798). The second, to the design of William Hill of Leeds, was opened at the corner of Edward Street on 14 May 1869. It finally closed in 1969, and though Councillor Harry Walker proposed that it should become a supplementary museum, it was demolished. The site was landscaped and has recently been redesigned (in 1998), with the capitals from the original building's four Corinthian columns preserved on the site. Ebenezer Chapel (see p. 64) can be seen in the background just beyond the Town Hall.

The first Stockport Grammar School was founded in 1487 under the will of Sir Edmund Shaa, who was born at Dukinfield in the parish of Stockport. Shaa was the Goldsmith and Court Jeweller to three monarchs: Edward IV, Richard III and Henry VII and was Mayor of London in 1482. It is thought that the first 'grammar school' teaching took place in the Parish Church but accommodation was later acquired in Chestergate. The school moved to new premises at the corner of Greek Street and Wellington Road South in 1832. In 1916 a new, larger school was opened at Mile End and improvement and expansion has continued up to the present day.

These photographs are taken from a number of similar pictures pasted into a personal copy of Varley's *History of Stockport Grammar School* (1946) and date to around 1910. The upper one shows the view from Wellington Road South while in the lower one closer study reveals much about the attitudes and dress of the time. This Greek Street school was demolished in 1923, and the site was used for the War Memorial Art Gallery which was opened by HRH Prince Henry of Gloucester on 15 October 1925.

Next door to the Grammar School was the Technical School, founded in 1888 and paid for by private subscription. It was opened by the Mayoress, Mrs Joseph Leigh, on 8 November 1889 and provided instruction in art, joinery, metalwork and engineering, and also had a dyehouse. A new wing was opened in 1915 and the name of the school was changed to 'Stockport College of Further Education' in 1927. It was demolished in the early 1970s, but the four commemorative stones from the two periods of building, 1888–89 and 1913–15, were preserved and incorporated into the front wall of the new (present) college erected on the same site. It is understood that the weathervane was claimed by Stockport Museum! Note the old Grammar School at the far right. The photograph is pre-1915.

Greek Street Secondary School opened on 22 April 1910, to supplement a day school first established in a few rooms in the Technical School in 1908. Together they provided facilities for 470 boys and 290 girls. This picture was taken during the First World War when the school became a military hospital, as did other local buildings such as the Town Hall, Pendlebury Hall and the council schools at Hollywood Park, North Reddish, Alexandra Park and Vernon Park.

Stockport's National School, supported by the 'National Society for Promoting the Education of the Poor in the Principles of the Established Church', was founded in 1825 and opened in 1827. It was intended to accommodate, under one roof, all the scholars (more than 3,000 of them) from the town's many 'Established Church' schools. Built of brick with a polished stone façade, it had two schoolrooms, each measuring 104ft by 40ft. It is thought to have earned its nickname of the 'Penny Madhouse' from the fact that the first pupils paid a penny a week for their schooling. The building was demolished in 1902 and the Town Hall was later built on the site.

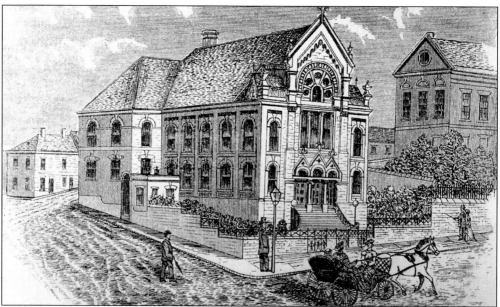

Ebenezer Chapel, seen here in an illustration from Heginbotham, was designed in Tudor Gothic style by T.H. Allen of Stockport and was opened in March 1882. It seated 650 people and there was a school adjoining. Eventually used for additional accommodation for the Town Hall, it was demolished in 1975. A grassy slope now covers the site. Note the end wall of the 'Penny Madhouse' at the right.

After the failure to acquire Underbank Hall as a Town Hall in the 1820s (see p. 30), the provision of a purpose built town hall, to centralize the town's scattered offices, was not considered until 1872, and it was not until 1904 that plans by Sir Alfred Brumwell Thomas were approved. The architect, born Alfred Thomas – adding 'Brumwell' in 1894 – was the son of Edward Thomas, surveyor to the district of Rotherhithe. He studied for three years at the Architectural Association in London. In 1898 he won a competition to design Belfast City Hall, which was opened by Lord Aberdeen in 1906, and was knighted; he died on 22 January 1948. The Town Hall's foundation stone was laid by the Mayor, Alderman Giles Atherton on 15 October 1904. The photograph shows the building under construction. The principal facade is 220ft long and 45ft high. In his book, *Edwardian Architecture: a Biographical Dictionary* (1985) A.S. Gray says, of the cluster of columns on the façade, that it 'is a design which would seem to derive from the Palais des Beaux-Arts at Lille'. The colonnaded clock tower, later described by Pevsner as 'too high and too heavy', rises to 130ft above street level. Its top stone, weighing almost a ton, was set in place on 30 January 1907. The builder of the Town Hall was Josiah Briggs of Heaton Norris, and it was opened by the Prince and Princess of Wales (later King George V and Queen Mary) on 7 July 1908.

Their Royal Highnesses, the Prince and Princess of Wales, accompanied by the Duke and Duchess of Westminster, arrived at Tiviot Dale station by special train from Chester at 3.20 p.m. After being greeted by the Mayor and Mayoress, Alderman and Mrs Henry Bell, and the Town Clerk, Mr Robert Hyde, the Prince inspected a Guard of Honour furnished by the 6th Cheshire Regiment.

Stands for the many spectators were erected in various places – here is the crowd in Tiviot Dale. Note the Christadelphian Church, in the background, (see p. 88).

More stands were provided in Mersey Square. It was estimated that over 6,000 schoolchildren were accommodated in the various stands. Note the fire station tower at the rear.

Here, Hillgate and the Underbanks are decorated, probably for the Prince of Wales' visit – note the feathers, top centre. Although the Royal procession took the easier route to and from the Town Hall – via Prince's Street, Mersey Square and Wellington Road South – the local shopkeepers took the opportunity to decorate all the main streets. Noticeable shops are, on the right: Amies bootmakers at 32 Little Underbank and Cragg and Walker's drapers at 34 and 36. Winter's clock is just visible on the left, through the decorations.

Here the royal carriage arrives at the Town Hall where a second Guard of Honour awaited the Royal couple. The opening ceremony was very brief and their Royal Highnesses were back at Tiviot Dale station for the train scheduled to leave for Chester at 4.40 p.m. At one hour and twenty minutes, it was a short visit indeed!

Alderman Henry Bell was Mayor of Stockport, 1906/7 and 1907/8, and is seen here with Mrs Bell. He was a member of the Bell's Brewery family and was much involved in local life, notably with the Stockport Vocal Union which he served for fifty-two years, first as treasurer then as honorary secretary, until 1929. Incidentally, the caption on this postcard is incorrect – Stockport only has a Mayor, not a Lord Mayor!

The town's worthies are posed here, outside the clearly recognisable Town Hall, to record their
efforts to raise funds for an extension to Stockport Infirmary in memory of the late King Edward
VII.

Stockport Infirmary, from a 'Valentine Series' postcard produced in the 1920s. In 1774 James
Briscall, a young surgeon, came to Stockport. His first consulting room was in a thatched cottage
on Churchgate, where the Thatched House public house now stands. He moved to a cottage at
Grapes Steps (see p. 36) and was later concerned with the opening of local public dispensaries.
He died in 1814, having made a great contribution to the progress of local medical treatment.
When larger premises were needed, Lady Vernon and Thomas Robinson gave adjacent plots
of land for the building of the Infirmary. It was founded in 1832 and opened on 24 and 25 July
1833; the architect was Richard Lane. A number of extra wings were added over the years. It
finally closed on 28 April 1996, when its services were transferred to Stepping Hill Hospital.
The site is presently awaiting redevelopment.

The Brentnall Street Day and Sunday Schools on Wellington Road South were designed by T.H. Allen of Stockport and opened on 27 May 1869. The Sunday school closed on 31 August 1930 and the building was rededicated as the Masonic Guildhall on 21 July 1932 by the Right Worshipful Brother C. Leicester-Warren, Provincial Grand Master for Cheshire. The building, described by Pevsner as 'Gothic to Jacobean-Asymmetrical', though still owned by the Freemasons, is now just designated as 'the Guildhall'. The illustration is from Heginbotham.

The Brookfield Hotel (left) on Wellington Road South began life as the Three Jolly Carters, licensed from at least 1838. The first Brookfield licence dates from 1867, the Brookfield Brewery having been established in Hempshaw Lane by the Marsland family in 1866. The frontage here bears a date stone '1898' and this Bullock Bros postcard possibly dates from around this time. The Brookfield is now occupied as business premises. Beyond the hotel is Bennett's Noted Bacon Shop at the corner of Cooper Street, and further on, at 205 Wellington Road South, is the premises of George W. Smith, coachbuilders. This company was here from the late 1880s and later progressed to car body building and engineering. The polygonal turrets of Trinity Wesleyan Methodist Chapel, founded 1886, are visible in the centre. The chapel was demolished in the 1970s, being replaced by a new church at Woodsmoor. Note the horse-drawn tram on the right, probably on the Hazel Grove service (see p. 54).

Six

Vernon Park, Portwood and Brinnington

In 1908 Vernon Park celebrated its Golden Jubilee. Its history begins in 1844 when a plot of land, known as Stringer's Fields, was given to the town by the Rt Hon. George John Warren, Lord Vernon, for 'public benefit'. The Council bought additional land in 1850, making a total area of 21 acres, and it was decided to develop it as Stockport's first public park. In 1857, under the supervision of the first Parks Committee, 47,000 trees and shrubs were purchased and the initial layout of the park began. Various local organizations donated plants, shelters, a fountain and a drinking water fountain. The park was officially opened by the Mayor, William Williamson, on 20 September 1858. In 1860 Vernon Park Museum was presented to the Borough by its MPs, James Kershaw and John Benjamin Smith, and it was extended in 1866. A bandstand was erected in 1888, with glasshouses and a conservatory in 1904. The first bowling green opened in 1905 and the second in 1908. The recreation ground dates from 1908 and the rock garden from 1935/6. The illustration is taken from a coloured postcard in the 'Grenville Series, St Peter's Square'. Part of the message on the back reads: 'Dear Brother, Just a p.c. to let you see how prettie [sic] the Park was at its Jubilee. The landscape bed was arrange[d] with lovely little plants in full blume [sic] … from your sister Annie'. The park is designated Grade II on English Heritage's *Register of Historic Parks and Gardens*, and is presently being upgraded over a three-year period after receiving Lottery funding.

This view of the Rose Garden is signed 'I. Ninnim' and was sent to an address in Idle, Bradford, Yorkshire. It is postmarked 'Stockport, 10 May 1947'.

A 'Fieldings (Stockport) Limited' postcard view of the Rock Garden and pools. Postmarked 'Stockport, 14 August 1953', it was sent by 'Edith and Tom' to an address in Ontario, Canada.

Crossley's café was removed from Rostron's Brow in the Market Place (see p. 16) and re-erected as part of the aviary in the park. The aviary was burned down by vandals in 1948.

The 'Roman' road, a somewhat narrow thoroughfare, runs through the park between the museum and the bowling greens. It was apparently once known as Royle's Lane and is thought to be the route used by Bonnie Prince Charlie on his retreat through Stockport to Manchester in 1745.

This postcard of Brinnington Rise, from the 'Grenville Series', is undated and, with no address or signature, bears the cryptic message: 'This is where I am now!'. The view shows the abrupt end of the tramlines. The Stockport Corporation Tramways Act 1900 gave permission for a double length of track, 123 yards long, to be laid along Great Portwood Street from a point 13 yards from its junction with Carrington Road. It ended at the Borough boundary – literally – and this really was the end of the line! It opened in 1901.

Another Brinnington view from a 'Twyford Series' postcard, printed in Bavaria, but unfortunately undated.

St Paul's Church, Portwood, was designed by Bowman and Crowther and built 1849–51 in the Perpendicular style. Some of the church's stained glass came from Brinnington Manor House. Dating from 3 July 1963, this photograph shows the spire being removed. The last service took place on 8 August 1971 and was followed almost immediately by the closure of the graveyard. After the church closed a painting entitled 'Rabboni', by Herbert Schmalz, presented to the church in 1923 by Captain Tom Nevill, the then owner of Bramall Hall, was given to the Hall where it can now be seen in the chapel. St Paul's was demolished in 1974.

This photograph of the interior of St Paul's was taken in the church's last days and shows the altar, flanked by St Paul and St Peter. The altar rails commemorated Lt Tom Rathman Mills, 6th Battalion, Manchester Regiment (TF), who was killed in action in the Dardanelles on 10 June 1915, aged twenty-eight. A Memorial Service was held at St Mary's Parish Church at 1 p.m. on Sunday 20 June. The altar rails, presented to St Paul's by Mr and Mrs T.H. Mills, of White Bank House, Brinnington, were first used on 9 January 1916.

In 1848, as Portwood's growing population had only one small Methodist New Connexion Chapel to serve it, the Wesleyan Methodists built Brunswick Chapel, seen here. Designed by James Wilson FSA of Bath, the chapel accommodated 770 people and cost £2,530. The chapel and burial ground closed in 1955 and the chapel was demolished. The burial ground now forms part of the Portwood traffic island, which is landscaped with paths and subways leading to local thoroughfares.

Brunswick Chapel Walking Day, around 1911. The procession is in the Charlotte Street/ Carrington Road area.

The first Portwood Wesleyan Day School was founded in 1858. The architect was again James Wilson. It was described as a handsome building with a bell turret, having six classrooms downstairs and one larger room upstairs. On the morning of Tuesday 28 February 1860, the headmaster, Mr Joseph Farnsworth, was upstairs with 100 children, and Miss Hall and several junior teachers were downstairs with 320 children, when a hurricane hit the town. At 11.30 a.m. a chimney near the bell turret collapsed, demolishing part of the roof, which the wind then lifted off and dropped, partly blocking exits. The children upstairs managed to get downstairs while the teachers below began to evacuate the rest. The school had been virtually destroyed within 15 minutes. Local firms rushed to send help to the stricken school, but unfortunately, seven children, aged from four to twelve years, had various injuries, and one four-year-old was killed outright. An inquest on 1 March recorded a verdict of accidental death, but severely criticized the building work. The school was rebuilt and Joseph Farnsworth stayed on until he retired in 1899, having been headmaster for forty years. The school became Portwood Day School when it was taken over by the Local Education Authority in 1912. The photograph dates from 1927 and shows a class of (about) five-year-olds, although not all the names could be recalled. Left to right, back row: -?-, -?-, -?-, Anne Heywood, Nona Pilkington, Elsie Platt, Edith Gee. Second row: -?-, Eileen Firbank, Bertha Ainscough, -?-, ? Hawley (twin), Monica Hawley, ? Hawley (twin). Third row: -?-, -?-, Emily Dawson, -?-, Mary Ogden, -?-, Joan Cunliffe. Front row: Doris Dean, Dorothy Upton. The rebuilt school which they all attended has only recently been demolished.

Vernon Park Day School, with accommodation for 920 scholars, was opened in January 1909, the year that school medical inspections were introduced. This photograph, from 1929, shows a class of forty-four girls with their teacher, Miss Greatorex (whose father was headmaster of Christ Church School, Heaton Norris) and headmaster Mr Hughes seated at the right. We have only a few scholars' names: On the back row, sixth from the left is Elsie Platt (?), with Gertrude Hough seventh from the left; Monica Hawley and Nona Pilkington are on the third row from the back, immediately next to Mr Hughes. On the front row, Norma Rogerson is fourth from the left, with Doris Dean and Vera Walton at the extreme right. Some of these girls appear in the photograph on the facing page.

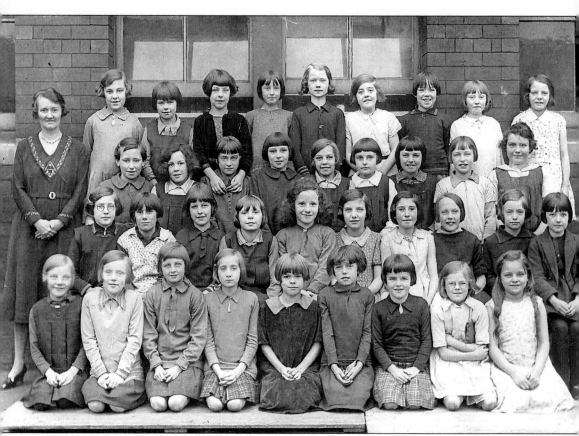

Girls growing up (readers may like to compare the faces here with those in the previous photographs). The girls are in the care of class teacher Miss Mabel Deaville at Vernon Park School in 1930. Left to right, back row: Doris Dean, Emily Dawson, Annie Scarlett, -?-, Hilda Pickles, Mary Ogden, Hilda Boyd, Evelyn Jemison, Nona Pilkington. Second row: -?-, Doris Nuttall, Elsie Brown, Marjorie Wilson, Gertrude Hough, Betty Derwent, -?-, -?-, -?-. Third row: Elsie Platt, -?-, Margaret Hawley, Annie Heywood, Bertha Ainscough, Dorothy Upton, Joan Cunliffe, Monica Hawley, -?-, -?-. Front row: -?-, Vera Ramscar, -?-, Norma Rogerson, Edith Gee, -?-, ? Murray, -?-, ? Walton. We are grateful to Miss Doris Dean for the gift of this and the previous four photographs. In spite of failing eyesight and the passage of time she has done a remarkable job in recalling so many former classmates.

This photograph of Portwood Gasworks was taken in September 1976. The Council bought the site of the old Portwood Reservoir in 1838 and apportioned it between the Gas and Manorial Tolls Committees. In 1878 the new Portwood Gasworks, designed by Mr Jacques, the engineer, were opened. The Portwood Cattle Ground and Department for Cleansing, which occupied the rest of the site, opened in the following year. The Millgate Gasworks closed in 1895 as gas manufacture was being centralized at Portwood. In 1931 the cleansing depot moved to Booth Street, Edgeley, to allow extensions to the gas and electricity departments. A waterless gas holder, 255ft high, with a capacity of three million cubic feet, was erected. The gasworks site was partially vacated in 1988 to make room for the Peel Centre which accommodates Sainsbury's Homebase and many other stores.

THE Quickest and the Cheapest Heat is obtained from Gas

A gas advertisement from the 1930s.

This is a close-up view of one of the cattle market gateposts which were removed during redevelopment.

This mid-1970s photograph shows the electricity cooling tower and Faulder's Mill. Henry Faulder & Co. began in the mid-1880s as wholesale English fruit preservers and confectioners, with premises at Bridge Street, Stockport, and at Heaton Norris. By 1906 they had taken over Warren Street Mill (shown here), formerly a cotton mill, as cocoa and chocolate manufacturers; they were also making jam and marmalade at Norris Bank, and confectionery at the Squirrel Works, Hallam Street, Heaviley. The jam and marmalade interest seems to have been abandoned around 1910. The Warren Street and Hallam Street businesses continued into the 1920s but only the Squirrel Works survived after the Second World War. Warren Street Mill was demolished in 1989.

The Stockport Corporation electricity works in Millgate opened in 1900 and were altered over the years, especially in 1931 when this extension was opened on 1 October. The cooling tower (see p. 81), along with the entire complex, was demolished in 1983.

An electricity advertisement from the 1930s.

Seven

Tiviot Dale and Lancashire Hill

Wesleyan Methodism had been introduced into Stockport by John Bennet of Chinley around 1740, and with an expanding congregation the officials of the old Park Chapel sought a piece of land on which to build a church large enough to meet the present and future demand. Designed by Richard Lane and opened in September 1826, Tiviot Dale Methodist Church, seen here in Heginbotham's illustration, became known as 'The Cathedral of Methodism in the North'. It seated 1,200 people and cost £12,000. Donations and collections taken at the opening services reduced this debt to £7,000 and by 1855 all debts had been cleared, despite the cost of additional roofing. There was even enough money for a minister's house to be built on Dodge Hill. The church's final service was held on 11 July 1971 and it was then demolished and replaced by a modern building, opened in 1972, which stands on what was the graveyard. There had been some 3,000 burials here and these were removed to the Borough Cemetery. A modern office block now stands on the site of the old church.

This rear view of the church, taken in July 1971, shows how it stood on the rocks which form the bank of the river. Parts of the riverbank nearby have since been remodelled for new road works.

This photograph was taken at about the time of the last service. The noticeboard advertises 'Rev. A. Connop, MBE. Interviews each Monday Evening from 6.30 p.m.'. The souvenir from the Second World War – E.W.S. – (Emergency Water Supply) – painted on the front wall is no longer visible. Pendlebury Hall was used for services between 1971 and '72 while the new church was being built.

The Buck and Dog, an old-established coaching house seen here in July 1977, had been remodelled or rebuilt in 1891. Members of the Shawcross family held the licence from the early 1820s to the 1850s. The pub had an ornate carved entrance which was fortunately saved when the pub was demolished in the 1980s Warren Street development scheme.

This 1891 doorcase, photographed in 1995, was cleaned and reused in the side wall of Barclays Bank on the same site. Nearby is an inscription recording the level reached by the flood waters of the River Mersey on 17 August 1799. This used to be set in the pub's side wall overlooking the river and had been placed there by the landlord of the time, James Brown. The plaque has since been moved several times and the original height is now unknown.

Tiviot Dale station was built on land once occupied by Mrs Elizabeth Hume, whose husband had owned a print works near the river. The site was bought by the Stockport, Timperley and Altrincham Junction Railway, later absorbed by the Cheshire Lines Committee. The station opened on 1 December 1865 and served the line running from Woodley to Altrincham. Between 1880 and 1902 it was also used by the Midland Railway's Manchester to London service, but gradually declined in importance after 1902 when the Midland Railway opened the alternative route via Cheadle Heath and the Disley Tunnel to New Mills South Junction, although local ramblers still used it. It closed in January 1967. The photograph dates from the mid-1960s.

Looking west along the tracks with St Mary's Roman Catholic Church (centre left, with the bell turret) on Roman Road in the mid-1960s. This area was formerly known as Higson's Brow, named after Joseph Higson (1759–1827) who lived on the Brow. Nearby, his small two-roomed cotton factory, with a cellar, was later the basis of a Roman Catholic Church opened in 1867. The present church, designed by Pugin and Pugin, dates from 1897. The Christadelphian church, seen just below St Mary's, began as Stockport High School and was built in 1857 by Major Henry Coppock, who objected to the religious teaching at the Grammar School. The High School only lasted about three years. The Christadelphians used it for a few years from 1875, then it became a Synagogue until 1902, when the Jewish congregation moved to Chestergate and the Christadelphians took it over again.

Another photograph from the mid-1960s, with Pendlebury Hall in the background (right). Ralph Pendlebury, born in Bolton, became a Stockport mill owner. Elected a councillor in 1837 and Mayor in 1838, he was knighted in 1840 for his handling of the town's Chartist troubles. He died in 1861, leaving a fortune of £100,000 to establish an orphanage. Relatives contested the will and after settlement the amount was reduced to £76,641. The trustees waited until interest on the money brought the amount back to its original figure, which is why the building, designed by Beaumont, dates from twenty years later, when only four of the original nine trustees were still alive! It has been a day and evening school, a hospital (see p. 63) and a temporary church, but never an orphanage. Although it is a listed building, it was allowed to deteriorate and was in danger of demolition, but it has fortunately been restored and is now a private nursing home.

The M63 motorway opened on 26 July 1982 and at this point covers the site of the former Tiviot Dale station, demolished in 1968. The motorway has recently been re-designated M60. The photograph, with Pendlebury Hall and St Mary's Roman Catholic Church still part of the skyline, was taken on the day before the opening.

The former Cheshire Lines Committee line was under snow in the cutting between Wellington Road North and Lancashire Hill in March 1969. St Mary's Roman Catholic Church can be seen at the top left. The M60 now runs along here but a tunnel through the sandstone rock face can still be seen.

Before the construction of Lancashire Hill, in 1794, the main road from Manchester ran down Dodge Hill and Old Road to Tiviot Dale, turning right and crossing Lancashire Bridge into the town. In this photograph of Dodge Hill, Roman Road is at the left. Roman Road is supposedly named for St Mary's Roman Catholic Church nearby. The old Tiviot Dale Church can be seen at the bottom of the hill, thus dating the photograph to not later than 1971. Note the road surface – modern setts, nearer the camera, adjoin the more traditional cobbled section.

Hanover Chapel, Lancashire Hill, built on what had been Raffald's Garden, was opened in 1821 and closed in 1962. During the centenary celebrations, in 1921, a new vestibule was added and Messrs Marples of Heaton Moor furnished the church parlour and minister's vestry and carpeted the rostrum and communion dais. A 'neat and artistic' baptismal font in solid oak was designed and made by Mr H. Sheperdson. The picture was taken not long before demolition in 1966/67. Note the entrance to Shottin's Court, and the scooters – all the rage at that time!

The interior of Hanover Chapel, undated.

Revd Nathaniel Knight Pugsley was born in Kentisbury, Devon, in 1787 and was educated at Hoxton College. He first came to Stockport in July 1815 as a temporary minister at Orchard Street Chapel (see p. 41). After returning to college he was invited to take over at Orchard Street, being ordained pastor there in 1816. He resigned in 1819, distressed by disagreements between the trustees and deacons. Shortly afterwards he was invited to be pastor of a new chapel yet to be built – Hanover Chapel – for which donations of £3,000 had already been offered. The chapel opened amid great rejoicing, and went from strength to strength. According to his obituary notice, he 'presided over a united and peaceful church' until age forced his retirement in 1858. He 'continued to cherish a warm interest' until his death at Meadow Bank, Stockport, on 5 June 1868; he was buried at Hanover Chapel.

Part of one of the gravestones in Hanover burial ground. Philip Chetham, the son of a yeoman, was born at Adswood Old Hall on 29 January 1788. He joined the Royal Navy at the age of fourteen, as a volunteer of the first class, on HMS *Phoebe*. Although present at Trafalgar, he did not actually participate in the battle. After three years in the Navy he went into business. He was installed as a Freemason in the Lodge of Peace (then No. 404) at the Coach and Horses, Newbridge Lane, on 3 October 1811. He became Worshipful Master in 1841. He married Johanna Clarke of Mevagissey, Cornwall, and they had a large family. 'Father Philip' as he was affectionately known, spent the latter part of his life at Newton Street, Edgeley, where he died on 19 July 1884 in his ninety-seventh year, the oldest Freemason in England.

This is an unnamed Court archway, on Lancashire Hill, around 1966; there were a number of similar ones in this area. This type of building coped admirably with Stockport's hilly terrain: dwellings were built around an open space, entering low at one side and climbing up to the higher street at the opposite side. Note especially here the variations in the brickwork, the stone footings and the setts leading into the courtyard.

A good view of the same courtyard is afforded from just inside the archway. The steps across the yard lead to a similar archway and to the street beyond.

In 1820 William Nelstrop rode on horseback from Ackworth, near Wakefield, to set up as a corn merchant in Stockport and founded his own company. In 1826 he married the daughter of William Oldfield, a local miller. He was Mayor of Stockport in 1841. Nelstrop's Albion Mill (1820) was ideally placed, close to the main route into Manchester, as well as the canal. It was expanded in the late 1860s, but was destroyed by fire in April 1893, as the picture records. The public loo made a 'convenient' vantage point for onlookers! The rebuilt mill, seen below in the late 1960s, is still operating.

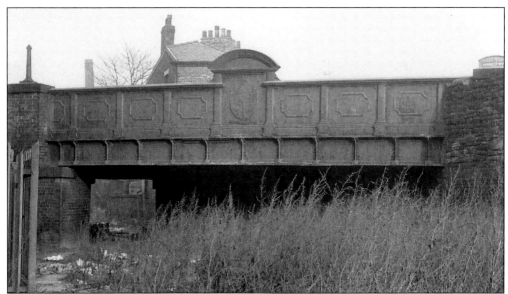

In 1793 the Manchester, Ashton and Oldham Canal Company were given leave to construct a short branch canal through Openshaw, Gorton and Reddish to Lancashire Hill, Heaton Norris. Opened in 1797, it was level throughout. It is hard today to imagine that, from the nearby canal terminus, a luxurious saloon boat used to set off for Manchester each morning at 9.30 a.m., returning at 4 p.m. Tuesdays and Thursdays – Cotton Exchange days – were especially busy. Many mills and factories were built along the banks. The canal ceased carrying commercial traffic in the early 1930s, but many older people remember swimming near the warm water outlets from the various mills. The picture shows the old canal bridge at the top of Lancashire Hill.

The canal closed altogether in 1962 and was filled in, but a trace survives in the name of The Navigation public house, formerly known as the Packet Boat. The pub has been remodelled since this photograph was taken in the 1960s.

Following the construction of Lancashire Hill – also known as Manchester Hill Road and/ or New Road – in 1794, and the coming of the canal in 1797, the area developed rapidly. Numerous public houses served the local community and travellers alike. The Nicholson's Arms was licensed to John Dodge in 1831, although the frontage shown here is obviously later. Note Hanover Chapel in the centre background of this view from 1966/67 when the demolition of most of Lancashire Hill's buildings took place.

In this slightly later picture, the old Nicholson's Arms is dwarfed by the modern high-rise flats which replaced the older houses and courtyards. A new modern public house has since replaced this one. The noticeboard reads R. Whipp, Builders, Ltd, Hyde.

There are few references to the Millstone public house, Lancashire Hill (not to be confused with the other Millstone at Portwood Place). The licensee in 1850 was Moses Chadwick. The Millstone closed in September 1967 and was demolished in the next month. Note the entrance to Higson's Yard, at the right.

The first mention of the Duke of Wellington public house is from 1831, when the licensee was John Antrobus. The frontage shown here dates from when the pub was rebuilt in 1899. The surrounding buildings were being demolished when this photograph was taken in 1967. Clarke's Brewery was founded by Richard Clarke in 1862 and became a limited company in the early 1880s. It had sixty pubs in Lancashire, Cheshire and Derbyshire, and was purchased by Boddington's in 1963 for a reputed £1 million. Notice also the arched entrance to Widow's Court (right).

Eight

The Heatons

Christ Church Parish was once part of the chapelry of St Thomas, Heaton Norris, itself formerly part of the Parish of Didsbury. Christ Church was founded in 1844. The church site, together with an endowment of £1,000, was the gift of Wilbraham Egerton Esq. and additional funds were raised by voluntary subscriptions, including: £7,000 from the Manchester and Eccles Church Building Society, £500 from the Chester Diocesan Society, £400 from the Incorporated Society for Building Churches, and £500 from Her Majesty's Commissioners. The church, designed by W. Hayley, was consecrated by John Bird, Bishop of Chester (later Archbishop of Canterbury) on 21 October 1846.

At the foundation ceremony, in 1844, it was announced that Mr Egerton had given £200 towards the cost of the spire, and Mr R.C. Sharp of Bramall Hall had promised a clock. Both spire and clock were damaged by the intense heat when a disastrous fire swept through the LNWR goods warehouse, on the opposite side of Wellington Road North, on 22 November 1877. The church itself was saved and the spire was later rebuilt. The photograph dates from 1969.

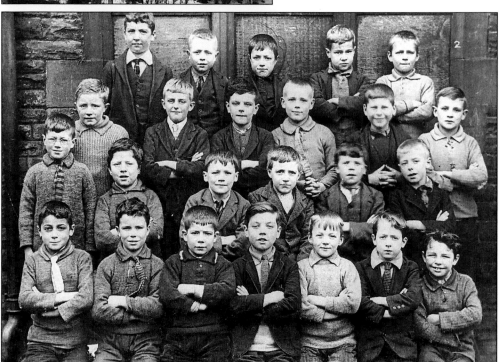

Christ Church's first rector was the Revd C.B. Jeaffreson; the Schools (1849) and Rectory (1854) were built during his incumbency. In 1877 the new rector, Revd James Bayley, made many improvements at his own expense, including the building of four new classrooms. The schoolchildren, pictured here around 1923, are unfortunately anonymous, apart from two boys in the second row from the back: first left is Jack Maguire and third right is Tom Goodwin.

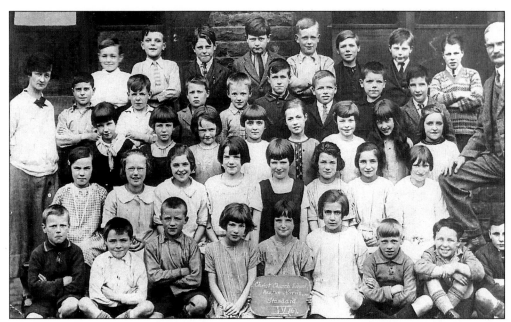

Here are the children of Standard IVb, around 1925, with their teacher, Miss Cornish, and headmaster, Mr Greatorex (see p. 79). Tom Goodwin is on the back row, fourth from the right. When he donated this and the previous photograph to the Stockport Historical Society's collection, Tom was elderly and almost blind, so no other faces could be recalled.

Christ Church became redundant in the early 1970s and the congregation moved to All Saints' – now designated Christ with All Saints. The Church Commissioners sold much of the woodwork – pews, screens, flooring, etc. – and the church was closed. Around 1976 the abandoned church was attacked by vandals who broke down the doors, smashed windows and caused other destruction both inside, as seen in the photograph, and outside, breaking gravestones and dumping rubbish. Finally, in November 1977, the wood in the roof was by some means set alight, and the body of the church was virtually burned out. Demolition work began in January 1978, but the tower and the spire were stabilized and preserved and are still a local landmark.

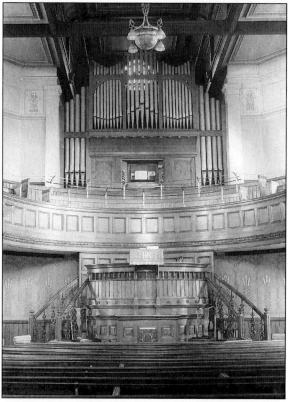

The new Primitive Methodist Chapel – Bethesda – was founded in June 1890, and the opening services were held on Thursday 5 March 1891. The architect was J.D. Mould of Manchester. Built by Josiah Briggs of Heaton Norris, the chapel seated 500 people. The Sunday School was in Bourne Street and opened in 1872. The day school, at the rear of the church, was missioned by John Penny and was popularly known as 'John Penny's School'. After the 'loyal service and devoted witness which characterized the history of Bethesda' (Closing Service Programme), the chapel was closed as part of an overall plan for the centralization of Methodist witness in Stockport. Final services were held on Sunday 10 September 1967. The building survives and is occupied as business premises.

This interior view of Bethesda chapel dates from about the time of the closure.

Heaton Moor Road, with the Plough Inn (first right) and St Paul's Church in the background, is seen here sometime before 1914. The gentleman walking in the road tips his hat to the lady cyclist. Next to the Plough Inn two telegraph boys are standing outside the shop/sub-post office.

This view of the corner of Heaton Moor Road and Shaw Road was taken around 1920. Directory entries for the Heatons are sparse but we do know that this shop, 1 Shaw Road, was occupied by William H. Mortimer, confectioner, in the mid-1880s, by William Pursglove, draper, in the mid- 1890s and by Cliff and Brown, drapers, in 1924. The style of window dressing, with goods on display from top to bottom, is typical of the early years of this century.

After Heaton Chapel station, seen here in a turn-of-the-century postcard, was opened in 1852, Heaton Moor Road gradually became built up. The small building at the right bears the name of F.S. Trueman whose coal, limestone and gravel business was based at Edgeley station from the early 1880s. The small branch office seen here is mentioned in directories up to 1893; the firm was still trading from Edgeley station in 1939.

Postmarked 'Stockport, 17 September 1909' this postcard from Rutland House, Heaton Chapel, to an address in Buxton bears the message: 'The secret you mention on your postcard I will keep strictly and closely and will not mention it to anybody'!

The toll-bar at the junction of Wellington Road North and Manchester Road, Heaton Chapel, was erected in 1869 on the site of a previous toll-bar. The building later became a branch office of the District Bank. Note also the police box.

The toll-bar was the last surviving example of its kind in the district and was protected by an Ancient Buildings Preservation Order. On 31 March 1966, by which time it was a branch of NatWest, it was ruined when an 18-ton lorry, fully laden with sand, crashed into it. It was totally demolished the following day as the remains were unsafe.

The Midland Railway's line from Manchester to Stockport opened on 1 January 1880, with seventeen trains calling at Heaton Mersey station each day. A branch line to Cheadle Heath opened in October 1901. Passenger services ceased on 3 July 1961 and goods traffic finished on 7 October 1963. The photograph shows the station just prior to demolition.

This photograph of Heaton Mersey village is always said to date from the late 1890s, but the letters 'E.R.' on the bottom right hand window would seem to indicate a date between 1901 and 1910. The picture shows some local inhabitants, including a telegraph boy, looking towards the camera. Alfred E. Cooper is known to have traded as a grocer in Love Lane, Heaton Norris, in 1893, and by 1899 he had a grocer's shop and post office at 101 Didsbury Road.

The children of Standard IV or V from St John's Church School, around 1909, contrast well with the girls of Fylde Lodge school (below) over fifty years later.

Situated at the corner of Mauldeth Road and Priestnall Road, and originally built as a private house, Fylde Lodge became a day and boarding school for girls in 1893. In 1921 Stockport Council rented the school and opened it as a High School for Girls, purchasing it for £2,500 in 1924. This photograph, showing some of the schoolgirls, is dated 1961/62. Left to right, back row: -?-, Elaine Simpson, Linda Williams (1), -?-, -?-, -?-, Christine Ollerenshaw, -?-, Sheila Evans. Middle row: -?-, -?-, Hilary Buckley, Christine Dods, -?-, -?-, -?, -?-, -?-, Marilyn Coppock, Kathleen Yates. Front row: Norma Derbyshire, Linda Turner, Gillian Edmunds, Sylvia Leadbetter, form mistress Mrs Stocks, Carol ?, -?-, Linda Williams (2) (the donor of this photograph – see also pp. 118 and 119), Noreen Rigby.

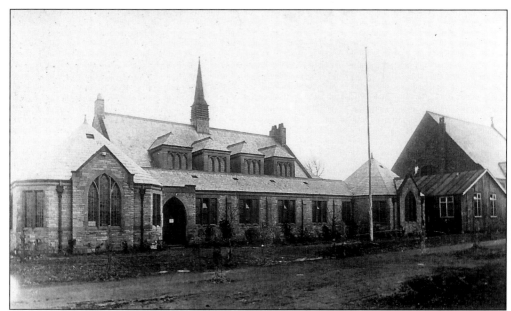

Heaton Mersey Methodist Church and Sunday School stood at the corner of Cavendish Road and Didsbury Road. The church was opened in February 1901, but from December 1914 to March 1919 its newly built schoolrooms were converted for use as a Red Cross Hospital for wounded servicemen. Heaton Moor Reform Club was also used as a hospital from 1917 to 1919. The church was demolished in September 1976.

This is a picture of the kitchen of Heaton Mersey Red Cross Hospital and is one of a series of postcards produced by Mr T. Everett Innes, a noted local photographer.

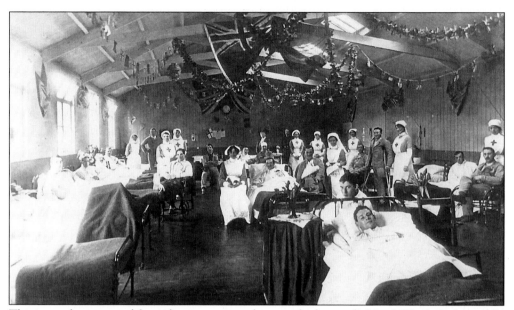

This is another postcard from the same series, showing the hospital's No. 2 Ward. A close study suggests that what appear to be Christmas decorations are actually augmented by various flags, so we cannot be certain of the nature of these celebrations.

Nurses and patients, with confirmation that in spite of their troubles, the men seem to have kept a sense of humour!

This photograph of the Club House, Heaton Norris, was taken in April 1978. Situated on Travis Brow, between Mount Pleasant and Huntsman's Brow, this pub's first recorded licensee was John Burgess in 1831. It had started as a beerhouse with its own brewhouse, becoming fully licensed when the Hat and Feathers in Heaton Lane was closed and its licence was transferred. The first Heaton Norris Petty Sessions were held here in 1838. It was demolished in the late 1970s as part of a new road development scheme from Didsbury Road to the M63, now the M60.

These gentlemen are the members of the Young Men's Bible Class at Baker Street Mission Church, around 1930. Most of them were remembered by name by Mrs Joan Thomas, Mrs Charlotte Riggs and Miss M. Gilbody – as they said, they *would* remember the men, wouldn't they?! Left to right, back row: -?-, George Stockley, ? Buckley, Tom Gregory, Stan Beech, Jack Shirt. Middle row: Jim Burgess, Joe Bath, Billy Bell, ? Briscoe, Tom Buckley, Joe Broster, Edwin Taylor, ? Holt, Jim Swindells. Front row: Harry Hooley, ? Maddocks, Harry Hall, Mr Stevenson (teacher, from Heaton Moor church), Harry Taylor, John Jackson. Baker Street was originally a mission church to Heaton Moor Congregational Church, then became a Congregational church in its own right and is now Baker Street United Reformed Church.

Nine

Edgeley, Cale Green and Davenport

In 1794, when it was thought that Napoleon might invade England, many Stockport men joined the Volunteer Movement. Apart from being disbanded between May 1802 and late 1803, the volunteers continued until the peace of 1815. In 1859, when another French invasion was feared, a Stockport Regiment was formed and its six companies, together with others, were consolidated into the 4th Cheshire Battalion Rifle Volunteers in August 1860. Drilling began on vacant land at Greek Street and it was soon decided to provide an armoury and drill room. Designed by Henry Bowman, the Armoury opened in April 1862 – the illustration is taken from an old lithograph – with a bazaar attended by Mr and Mrs Gladstone and what the *Stockport Advertiser* described as, 'the elite and *bon-ton* of the Borough and its suburbs'. It provided offices, a Regimental Institute, a bandroom and storage, with a drill hall which was 180ft long by 60ft wide. In 1887 the Regiment was renamed the 4th Volunteer Battalion, The Cheshire Regiment, and in 1907 became the 6th Battalion, The Cheshire Regiment (TF). The 'Territorials' are still based here.

The Church of Our Lady and the Apostles, Shaw Heath, designed by Edmund Kirby of Liverpool, was opened on 12 February 1905. Built in the Gothic style, of Ruabon brick, it consists of a chancel, nave, aisles, vestry and west porch, and seated 800 people. The Revd Canon Hugh McGeever (inset), born in Chester in 1870, educated in France and at Durham, was ordained in 1893, becoming curate at Stockport St Philip and St James for a year. After moving to Wrexham, he returned to Stockport in 1896, becoming rector of his old church in 1904. He became rector of Our Lady's in 1905 and was installed as a canon of the Diocese of Shrewsbury in October 1928. He was well loved, if strict, and renowned for walking about the parish hauling in backsliders to attend church. He died on 26 March 1934 after a year-long illness. There was a vast congregation for his funeral, with a choir of sixty priests to sing Requiem Mass. He is buried in the Borough Cemetery.

The staff of Hurst Brothers, printers, enjoy the works' picnic on Saturday 22 June 1912. John Hurst, the proprietor, is the whiskered gentleman at the right; others who have been identified in the picture are: Mr Barnes lying down at the left, and the lady with the dark bow at the neck of her blouse, to the left of centre, is Ruth Hutchins, who later became Mrs Barnes.

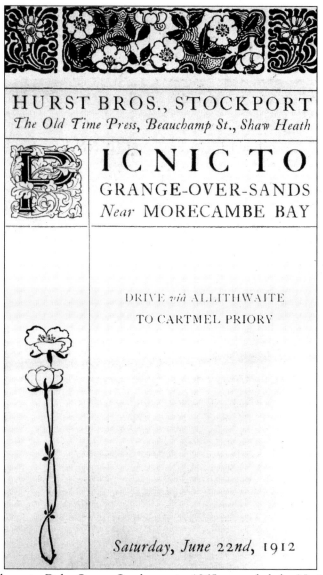

HURST BROS., STOCKPORT

The Old Time Press, Beauchamp St., Shaw Heath

PICNIC TO
GRANGE-OVER-SANDS
Near MORECAMBE BAY

DRIVE *via* ALLITHWAITE

TO CARTMEL PRIORY

Saturday, June 22nd, 1912

John Hurst was born in Duke Street, Stockport, in 1865, attended the National Day School (the 'Penny Madhouse') and from the age of ten worked as a half-timer, later becoming apprenticed to two different Stockport printers. He performed brilliantly in trade examinations and, in the 1890s, went into business with his brother William Gee Hurst in Mottram Street. By 1905 they had moved to Beauchamp Street. He was a noted local historian and his ten volumes of news cuttings, notes and photographs can be seen in Stockport Central Library's Heritage Library. He retired to Irby on the Wirral, in 1930, although he returned to Stockport after his wife's death, in 1944, to live with his daughter at 76 Vienna Road. He died on 24 January 1952, aged eighty-six. The business continued until the early 1970s. This is the title page for the picnic programme for 1912, a good illustration of the elegant art nouveau style of printing of the time, and an excellent example of the firm's high standards. Other pages describe the proposed route and give the menu for the day: Breakfast was fish, ham and eggs, bread and butter, jam, tea and coffee. For dinner there was soup, roast beef, roast lamb, mint sauce, vegetables and salads, Victoria pudding, blancmange, jellies and cheese etc.!

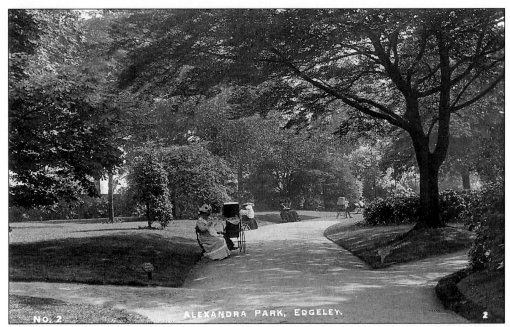

In 1908 the Corporation purchased the Edgeley House estate from Mr H.R. Sykes, to form Alexandra Park, named in honour of Queen Alexandra. Mr A.H. Sykes gave £500 towards the laying out of the park, whose 10 acres included bowling greens and tennis courts. The illustration is taken from an 'A.H. & S. Stockport, Branch Series' postcard.

The electric tram service from Stockport to Woodley opened in August 1901. This tram, seen in Castle Street/Edgeley Road in a 'Grenville Series' postcard, carries an advertisement for Stansfield, milliner/draper – there is an entry for Stansfield and Bleazard, milliners, in Lower Hillgate in a 1910 directory: is there possibly a connection? This card was used as a Christmas greeting, 'From T.B.'

Castle Street, Edgeley, from an undated 'A.H. & S. Stockport, Branch Series' postcard. The Royal Oak is at the left – the first known licensee was James Oakes in 1838. Duchy Street is at the right, and the wall carries numerous advertisements. Wood's, 60 Stretford Road, Manchester, are offering 'Lucky Wedding Rings, 22 carat gold' and a poster for the Ardwick Green Empire advertises James Learmouth's company in *The Station Master*. A manuscript index to the programmes at this theatre, in the Arts Library, Manchester Central Library, reveals that from 12 October 1914, Bob Stevens was in both *The Hairdresser* and *The Station Master* – the company's only productions there. Like the Stockport Theatre Royal (p. 53), the Ardwick Green Empire (1904) was designed by Frank Matcham. Ella Retford, whose name is in large letters at the bottom of the poster, was a vaudeville and pantomime actress who died in 1962, aged seventy-six. The song 'Won't you come home, Bill Bailey?' is said to be associated with her.

This illustration comes from an undated, but probably pre-1914, 'Grenville Series' postcard. Here, the Royal Oak is at the right, so giving an interesting round-the-corner view from the previous picture. The spire of St Matthew's Church in Grenville Street can be seen above the rooftops at the right.

St Matthew's Church was built on land donated by Robert Gee of Holly Wood (House) and was designed by J.S. Crowther. This was the second church he designed as an independent architect. It was opened in 1858 and the tower and spire were added in 1866. Here, the children of the Sunday school, complete with banner and flowers, prepare for Walking Day in 1914, with no hint of the impending hostilities.

The ladies of the church exhibit a variety of costumes on the same occasion; there are many transitional styles covering Victorian, Edwardian and more modern times.

This 'A.H. & S.M.' postcard, undated view of Edgeley Park, shows a view of one of the smallest, but at the same time one of the prettiest, of Stockport's parks. It was the gift of Captain T.H. Sykes and Mr A.H. Sykes and opened on 1 May 1889. It originally covered $1\frac{1}{4}$ acres, although the Corporation later added 2 more acres, an extension which was opened on 2 May 1903.

An undated 'Grenville Series' postcard view of the boating facilities on one of the reservoirs within the park. The card is endorsed: 'The old, old path' but has no addressee or sender's name.

Linda Williams and her brother Ian pose outside the family home at 94 Brinksway Road, around 1953. In correspondence Linda (now Linda Lewis and living in Australia) remembers regularly climbing up Lark Hill to Edgeley: 'was it really so steep?'. She also remembers the River Mersey at the back door, and the 'dark and cold' coal cellar. Across the road can be seen part of the Pictorium (left), and the premises of P. & L. Foster (right), sheet metal workers, at 103 Brinksway Road.

The Brinksway Pictorium was purpose built as a picture house around 1915. A correspondent to the *Stockport Advertiser* in 1978 recalled that 'the piano was concealed behind a curtain at the front of the screen … [and] … the light for the music stand was a lower power bulb with a metal shade …'. Closed as a cinema in 1958, it was occupied as business premises and this photograph, from July 1976, bears the traces: Brinksway trade warehouse, clearance lines, etc. Destroyed by fire in January 1978, it was finally cleared away later that year. Note the two frontages, and also the fact that, when compared with the picture above, the building at the corner of Lark Hill, at the right of the cinema, has lost its chimney.

A Brinksway Sunday school concert, 1951/52. Lyn Chapman is seated on the front row, third from the left, while fourth from the left is Linda Williams. Second from the right, on the front row is Jennifer Powell and third is Joan Mellor. On the next row Jean Broadhead is fourth from the left, behind Linda, while fifth from the right is Barbara Lees. Others in this group include Jennifer Powell's sister Joan (?), Margaret ?, Beverley Williams and her brother David(?) or Geoffrey (?). Perhaps some readers may recognize themselves.

Hollywood Park Primary School, opened in 1907, had accommodation for 700 children. Here, in June 1952, Linda Williams is third from the right on the second row from the front, while Beverley Williams is fourth from the right in the middle row.

Mrs Esther Harriet Burns and her husband James opened the Electra Cinema in Cheadle in 1912. Widowed in 1926, Mrs Burns continued in the business and opened the Forum at Wythenshawe in 1934. However, both of these cinemas were sold to the ABC Circuit in 1936 to raise funds to build the Davenport Cinema and Theatre on Buxton Road. Designed by Charles Hartley (Mayor of Stockport in 1947/48), the Davenport opened on 17 June 1937. Prices were: 1/6 for the circle, 1/3 in the balcony and 6d to 1/- in the stalls. A café and restaurant service was also provided. The programme for the opening night included a presentation by Millie Jackson's Streamline Six dancers, Harold Betts at the Compton organ, and a colour film of the Trooping of the Colour. The feature film was *The Man in the Mirror* starring Edward Everett Horton and Genevieve Tobin. In 1957, the complex was taken over by Jack Edge and used for cinema shows and stage productions, both amateur and professional. Latterly, the Davenport was owned by Stockport Grammar School. The 'Final Curtain' show, on Sunday 9 March 1997, was a Charity Gala performance featuring Bill Tarmey and Frank Carson. The building was demolished soon afterwards and at the present time (July 1998) the site is being redeveloped by the Grammar School.

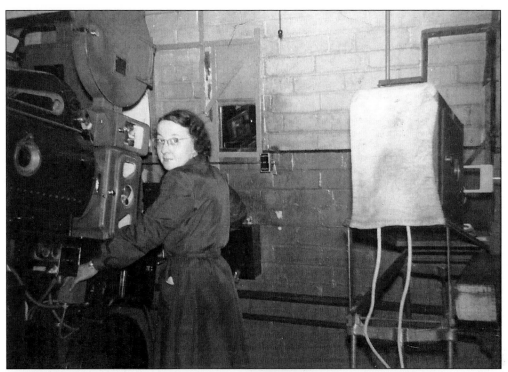

An unusual photograph of the projection room with projectionist Gladys Kennerley.

The organist, Harold Betts, was born Harold Rabetts. After playing at the Regent Cinema, Chatham, he joined Granada Theatres, appearing at the Granada in Bedford (1934), the Rialto in Leytonstone (1934–6) and the Electra in Bournemouth, before coming to Stockport to open the Davenport. Unfortunately, his later career is not known – can anyone help?

Frank Stafford Johnson, born in 1873, founded his own firm of cotton doublers in Melville Street in 1897 at the age of twenty-four (see p. 24). It became a limited company in 1930 and he became the governing director. Around 1900, after his marriage, he went to live in this house, 'The Paddocks' in The Crescent, Davenport. Built around 1880, it stood in its own grounds of some three acres; it had one grass and one hard tennis court, stables and other outbuildings. He was a keen sportsman, playing lacrosse for Cheshire and England and, as well as belonging to Stockport and Davenport Golf Clubs, he was a life member of Stockport Cricket Club. He also had a long association with Stockport Unitarian Church. Unfortunately, his wife died in 1919, leaving two sons and two daughters. In 1946 he moved to Bramhall, and he died at his home, 'Brynnington', Broadway, in April 1950, aged seventy-seven. The upper picture shows 'The Paddocks' viewed from the driveway; the lower picture is a view across one of the tennis courts.

Frank S. Johnson was one of the first people in the area to own a car. Here, he is seen in his AC 2-litre sports car, around 1923. (An AC 2-litre was the first British car to win the Monte Carlo Rally outright in 1926). This photograph was taken outside the stables and greenhouse and the 'passenger' is his dog 'Pip'.

'Pip' and a friend choose another form of transport! It is understood that Frank often travelled to business in his pony and trap, in spite of having a car and the pony could find its own way home!

Davenport Park was created out of Simpson's Farm, Mile End, at the end of the last century, and was named after the land's previous owners, the Davenport family of Bramall Hall. The park was in the township of Bramhall until it, and other parts of Bramhall, were incorporated into Stockport in 1901. By 1906 most of the houses had been erected, but the roads were still unmade and the Corporation's Highways Committee insisted that something should be done. As a result the residents set up the Davenport Park Roads Committee in August 1906. Each owner undertook to pay his share of the cost and the roads were surfaced in 1907. After ninety-two years the committee is still very active, though at some stage the word 'Roads' was dropped from the title. Today it deals with much more than road maintenance, particularly since the park became a conservation area in 1979. There are two entrances: one is from Buxton Road – this 'A.H. & S.M. Woodhey Series' postcard, dated to around 1910, shows the view from this entrance – and the other is from Bramhall Lane. Through-traffic is barred from the park and one entrance is kept closed. On one day in each year both entrances are closed to assert the residents' rights.

The Stockport, Disley and Whaley Bridge Railway opened its line from Edgeley to Whaley Bridge in 1857, with an extension to Buxton in 1863. Davenport station opened in 1858, having been provided at the special request of Colonel William Davenport of Bramall Hall. This postcard, postmarked 'Stockport, December 23 1904' was addressed to Miss B. Hooley, Mahood Street, Edgeley, with Christmas greetings 'from Lizzie and Harry'. Advertisements on the station include the *Daily Dispatch* and K Boots. Note the coalyard and wagons in the background, now the site of a car park.

Gustav Hamel left Cambridge University in 1910 and the next year obtained his Royal Aero Club Aviator's Certificate. He gave many displays all over the country, eventually coming to Stockport in 1913, as may be seen in the notice from the *Stockport Advertiser* below. Stockport's first experience of powered flight was on Thursday 4 September when Hamel took off from Mr Woodall's field at 4 p.m. for a flight lasting about 15 minutes; he made a second flight later that same day. On Saturday 6 September he made two more flights. During the afternoon visitors to the Horticultural Show at Bramall Hall 'had a splendid opportunity of witnessing the flights', one of which passed right over the showground. The *Advertiser* commented, 'we cannot but conjecture as to the possibilities of the art [of flying] and wonder'. This was an interesting statement, considering that by the end of the First World War, Stockport (Heaton Chapel) was the home of National Aircraft Factory Number One. Gustav Hamel, whose father was an English-naturalized German doctor who had attended the late King Edward VII and been awarded the MVO, flew the latest 80hp two-seater Bleriot monoplane. He died in 1914 while crossing the English Channel from France: his plane disappeared after take-off on 23 May and his body was found by a fishing vessel nearly two months later.

NEXT WEEK.   **NEXT WEEK.**

MR. GUSTAV HAMEL

The World-Renowned Airman, will give

FLYING AND PASSENGER CARRYING EXHIBITIONS

using his latest type 80-h.p. double-seater Bleriot Monoplane, at

GARNER'S LANE. ADSWOOD.

ON THE LAND OF MR. WOODALL, BATES LEY FARM,

Within a few minutes' walk of Davenport and Cheadle Hulme Stations, L. and N.W. Railway, and Tram Cars, on

THURSDAY AND SATURDAY, NEXT WEEK.

SEPTEMBER 4th and 6th.   Flights from 5 to 6·30 each day.

ADMISSION. Thursday, 1s.: Saturday, 6d.; Reserved Enclosure, 1s.: Motor Cars (including driver), 2s. Intending passengers may book a seat on the Flying Ground at the advertised times. Further particulars of GEORGE H. TUPLING, Whitchurch, Salop.

This is an advertisement for the forthcoming flying display of Gustav Hamel printed in the *Stockport Advertiser* on Friday 29 August 1913.

This delightful postcard in the 'Grenville Series' shows Adswood Lane East and Cale Green Post Office. The people are mostly watching the photographer, but the policeman, walking towards the little girl on the right, obviously has other things to do with his time.

Members of the Cale Green Reform Club pose outside their headquarters before taking a charabanc outing to – who knows where – in the late 1920s or early '30s. Note the monogram on the side of the charabanc. It may possibly represent William C. Henshaw's wheelwright and commercial vehicle body building business, begun in the town in 1836 by William's grandfather. In 1933 William C. Henshaw operated from the Stockport Body Works on Wellington Road South offering 'convertible bodies'.

Joseph Heginbotham worked for J. Woodrow, hat manufacturer, on Adswood Lane West. In March 1908 Mr Heginbotham resigned his position as manager, as the poem relates, after twenty-three years with Mr Woodrow. On 13 March, a week after the event recorded in the poem, Alderman Briggs presented Mr Heginbotham with 'a handsome dressing case with silver-mounted ebony fittings'. The case was inscribed: 'Presented by members of the Cale Green Conservative Club to Mr Joseph Heginbotham, President 1900-1-2-3-7-8'. The club was on Dundonald Street. Mr Heginbotham, accompanied by his wife, was going to tour the United States in an effort to restore his failing health. We have not been able to ascertain the outcome of the tour.

Presentation to Mr. J. Heginbotham.

Lines on his Resignation as Manager to Messrs. Woodrow, Ltd., Stockport ; and his Visit to America.

We are met here this evening to honour
  An old friend who is going away ;
After 23 years of good service,
  Well respected and esteemed, I can say.

We are all very sorry he is leaving,
  He has served us so well and so long ;
And we hope when he's finished his journey
  He'll return home, both healthy and strong.

Twenty-three long years in one hat shop
  Is a record to be proud of I'm sure ;
Doing duty between men and masters
  And especially those chaps that use lures.

It's a very queer trade is this hatting,
  Sometimes, both for masters and men ;
When there's trouble in all the departments
  One wishes they'd ne'er see it again.

On behalf of friends here this evening,
  I'm sure there's not the least doubt,
"Joe" leaves with our very best wishes,
  And we wish him a "champion out."

The gold watch we are here to present him
  Expresses our hearty good will,
The respect and esteem that we hold him,
  In a position very few can fulfil.

It's been subscribed for by men, women and masters,
  Jolly hatters both in silk and in felt ;
Let's hope he may long live to wear it,
  For I'm sure he'll ne'er want it to melt.

I hope, when he's crossing the ocean,
  This present will keep him in mind
Of the many dear friends in old England
  He is leaving so far behind.

I've no doubt, when he's crossed the Atlantic,
  He's sure to have a good time,
Among friends, relations, and Yankees,
  That will recall happy days of Lang Syne.

Then here's good health to "Joe" and his "missus"
  Who is going with him o'er the foam ;
We all wish them a jolly good outing,
  A nice passage and safe welcome home.

March 6th, 1908.   H. WHITTAKER.

– and finally!